Norman and June Buckley have nearly 20 years
experience in researching and writing guidebooks, both
in Britain and continental Europe. They are keen
walkers and many of their books focus on footpaths
and other routes for walkers.

Norman is a keen environmentalist with qualifications in
Environmental Management and an M.A. in Lake District Studies.
June also holds qualifications in Tourism.
East Anglia has long been a favourite area and they have made
many visits over the years. This comprehensive
Visitor Guide follows Norman's *Guide to the Lake District*,
also in this series.

Published by

Landmark Publishing
Ashbourne Hall, Cokayne Ave, Ashbourne,
Derbyshire   501 405 455

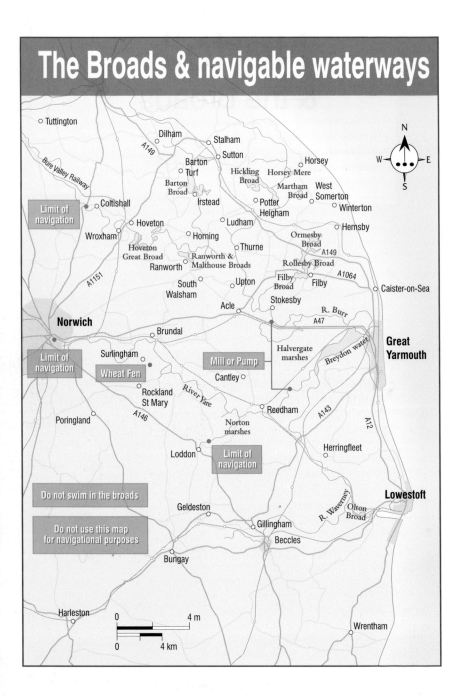

The Broads & navigable waterways

Tuttington

Dilham

A149

Bure Valley Railway

Stalham

Sutton

Barton Turf

Hickling Broad

Horsey Mere

Horsey

West Somerton

Martham Broad

Coltishall

Barton Broad

Irstead

Potter Heigham

Winterton

Limit of navigation

Hoveton

Ludham

Hemsby

Wroxham

Horning

Thurne

Ormesby Broad

A149

Hoveton Great Broad

Ranworth & Malthouse Broads

Rollesby Broad

A1064

A1151

Ranworth

Filby Broad

Filby

Caister-on-Sea

South Walsham

Upton

Stokesby

Acle

R. Bure

A47

Norwich

Brundal

Great Yarmouth

Limit of navigation

Surlingham

Mill or Pump

Halvergate marshes

Breydon water

Wheat Fen

Cantley

Rockland St Mary

River Yare

A146

Reedham

A143

A12

Poringland

Norton marshes

Loddon

Limit of navigation

Herringfleet

Lowestoft

Do not swim in the broads

Geldeston

R. Waveney

Olton Broad

Do not use this map for navigational purposes

Gillingham

Beccles

Bungay

Harleston

0   4 m

0   4 km

Wrentham

N
W   E
S

Norfolk
& the Broads

Norman and June Buckley

Boats at Potter Heigham

Contents

Maps

Welcome to
Norfolk and the Broads

Bulging out into the North Sea, flanked by a long coastline, the predominantly low-lying land which makes up Norfolk and most of East Anglia has always been a water-dominated landscape. Rivers have never flowed swiftly and purposefully to the sea; they crawl along as if reluctant to give up their waters to the flat, marshy, estuaries, traditionally subject to flooding in prolonged or violent wet weather. From Roman times much energy, time and money has gone into elaborate schemes of drainage, winning back thousands of rich alluvial acres from the water.

More dramatic is the sea's confrontation with the coast which is, for the most part, vulnerable with, at best, low,

Top Tips

- **The Broads**
  Supreme for water-based holidays

- **Norwich**
  One of Britain's finest cities

- **The north Norfolk coast**
  Holiday resorts and as well unspoilt scenery, with wonderful nature reserves

- **Historic towns and delightful villages**

- **World-class visitor attractions in profusion**
  Sandringham, Blickling Hall, Felbrigg Hall, Castle Acre Priory, Bressingham, Pensthorpe, Oxburgh Hall, Holkham Hall, Thetford Forest

- **Lord Nelson**
  A Norfolk man

- **Steam railways**

- **Country walking**
  Peddars Way, Angles Way, North Norfolk Coast Path

- **Characteristic and attractive village signs**

Brick Nogging

Brick infilling between the uprights of timber-framed buildings. Sometimes, nogging was used to replace earlier wattle and daub, as the craft of daubing died out and bricks became cheaper and widely available.

Sometimes the brickwork is arranged in patterns: herringbone, chevron, horizontal or vertical.

crumbling cliffs. Here, the conflict takes two forms. Firstly there is the constant erosion, the creeping destruction caused by the ceaseless pounding at dunes, soft cliffs and modern sea defences, gaining possession of land, villages and the occasional town over the centuries. The prime example is Dunwich in Suffolk, progressively reduced from a considerable town, bishopric and major port to the present minor village by this elemental power. Secondly, the unfortunate combination of tides and winds can produce the 'North Sea Surge', with enormous tidal waves bursting through the defences, as in 1953 when much low-lying land in East Anglia was flooded, with great loss of life and property.

There is, however, a certain amount of give and take in the relationship between land and sea. Over a long period of time, silting has extended the North Norfolk coast into the Wash; former little ports such as Blakeney and Cley next the Sea are now some distance inland. Similarly, the large town and port of Great Yarmouth has been built on a spit of land which has grown steadily since medieval times.

The final element in this watery landscape is the Norfolk (and Suffolk) Broads. Extensive digging of peat for fuel from Anglo-Saxon times to the early fourteenth century produced shallow but wide pits which, inevitably, flooded, producing the series of lakes and their connecting waterways which play a large part in today's East Anglian holiday economy.

On the whole, East Anglia is not noted for spectacular geology. There are no thrusting mountain ranges, no glens, ravines or similar landscape features. Apart from the cliffs at Hunstanton, all is quietly understated. Most noteworthy is a broad band of chalk which crosses southern England diagonally, from Dorset to those cliffs at Hunstanton, producing a gently rolling countryside which, at its highest a few miles southwest of Bury St Edmunds in Suffolk, reaches a maximum of 125m (410ft). To the west of the chalk lie some of the oldest East Anglian strata, beds of Gault, Greensand and Kimmeridge Clay, whilst to the east Red Crag and Forest Beds have deposits of the Pliocene Age, including historically valuable seashells.

Despite the threats posed by water, the area has long proved attractive to man. In prehistoric times access to this isolated area from the rest of England was difficult; the great watery barrier of the Fens extended south almost as far as today's Cambridge and most of what is now Essex was covered in dense forest. The most attractive route was to use the chalk ridge to infiltrate into Breckland (see Chapter 4). Here, forest was relatively easy to clear and the light, sandy soil was easier to work than the heavy clays elsewhere in the area. This became one of the country's most densely populated areas, with crop growing and cattle grazing to excess over the centuries producing a heath area vulnerable to sand storms and overpopulated by rabbits, a state of affairs not remedied until the twentieth century with the arrival of the Forestry Commission and mass planting of trees for commercial purposes. A very early industry, digging out and shaping flints, developed at Grimes Graves. In prehistoric times these were used as tools and weapons; in medieval times they became an important local building material.

Well before the arrival of the Romans, the population had become organised into tribes; because of Boudicca's rebellion against the Romans, the Iceni were the best known of these. Following the departure of the Romans, waves of Angle, Saxon and Jute invaders crossed the North Sea to arrive on the accessible shores, settling throughout the

Pargeting

Pargetry, parget-work or parge-work are all terms used to describe ornamental designs in plaster, either relief or incised. At first, designs were simple, incised into the wet plaster with a stick or group of sticks tied into a comb or fan shape.

The craft reached its height in the 17th century.

area, developing agriculture, building churches, often with distinctive round towers, and burying special chieftains in great splendour, as at Sutton Hoo in Essex.

Despite the exploits of Hereward the Wake, the Norman Conquest eventually prevailed in East Anglia. Churches were now built in Norman style, often modifying the earlier Anglo-Saxon buildings, and the whole area thrived, so much so that at the time of the Domes-

Flint

That awkward local material, flint, is at the very heart of East Anglian church building, great and small, and also of many less exalted buildings. Nowhere in the world has flint been used so extensively for building as in Norfolk and adjacent counties. Look out for panels of dressed (knapped) flints which produce a patterned decorative effect known locally as 'flushwork', arranged with limestone or brick into decorative patterns in walls throughout the area.

Flint is found in the chalk band, a strange stone, it is one of the purest forms of silica and so hard as to be virtually indestructible, yet it can be easily fractured in any direction. This makes it an awkward building stone, but means it can be chipped and polished to a sharp edge for use as axe heads, farming implements and weapons.

Grimes Graves, near Thetford is one of the world's earliest industrial sites. Neolithic people mined flint here on a site covering 37 hectares, using only tools such as deer antler picks, polished flint axes and wooden shovels they dug pits up to 12 metres deep to extract the flint from where it lay buried beneath the chalk.

day Book the population density was among the highest in England.

The greatest landscape changes, however, occurred some centuries later when the work of Vermuyden and others brought about enormous enhancement of the drainage of the still very extensive fen areas, straightening rivers, digging long, wide, drainage channels and pumping water from lower-lying fields into these channels. This achievement enabled agricultural pioneers such as Coke at Holkham and 'Turnip' Townshend of Raynham to transform much of East Anglia into probably the richest farming area in Britain, in the former case substituting wheat for the prevailing rye. There was also a side benefit in that naviga-tion to inland ports such as Wisbech, Peterborough and Bedford was much improved.

The small fields, which had been 'enclosed' long before the nineteenth-century Parliamentary Enclosure Acts, were expanded during the twentieth century by much destruction of old hedges, creating 'prairies' which enable large and expensive agricultural machinery to function more efficiently. The early enclosures also had a profound effect on the shape of many villages; the classic English 'nuclear' village results from the formerly commonly-owned fields being located around the outside of several closely grouped houses, whilst the East Anglian model arose when, several hundred years

**Great Yarmouth
Nelson Museum**

earlier then elsewhere, common fields were divided and the land was grouped according to ownership, with a house built centrally within each holding of land, producing a spaced-out, diffuse village.

Prior to the agricultural reforms of the eighteenth century, sheep ruled the East Anglian economy for some centuries, generating great wealth for many merchants. 'Wool' towns and villages competed in displaying this wealth, most usually by building churches of great stature and richly carved flamboyance, permanent monuments to a prosperous age. In creating monuments and, even more so, in the proliferation of vernacular architecture, the builders of East Anglia have left a wealth of distinctive features and techniques which add immeasurably to the attraction of so many of the town and villages. Timber framing with plastered wattle and daub or brick nogging infill and, in some surviving cases, overhanging upper storeys, mixes happily with colour-washed rendering, with or without the pargeting which is wonderfully decorative in a few instances. That awkward local material, flint, is at the very heart of the construction of churches both great and small and also of many less exalted buildings. Particularly good is the inclusion of panels of dressed flints within a structure to produce a patterned decorative effect known locally as 'flushwork'.

Although for centuries Norwich was second only to London as England's largest city, the rural traditions of Norfolk, coupled with the absence of coal or iron ore deposits – hence no industrial revolution – have discouraged the development of large cities and towns. There are no roads which go through the area to reach anywhere else. Apart from the fact that this precludes the formation of an M4-style 'corridor', it also has something to do with the distinctive character of Norfolk and its people. Norwich is much the biggest settlement, but is still of compara-

Nature Reserves

Norfolk with its long, low coastline jutting out into the North Sea, its slow rivers, marshes and of course, The Broads, is a paradise for bird watchers. Nature reserves are widespread throughout the area and too numerous to mention in total; lists are widely available in the area. The most important reserves are included in the relevant chapters. The reserves listed below are operated by the Royal Society for the Protection of Birds. All have hides and trails; some have more comprehensive visitor facilities. Most are open to the public at all times.

Snettisham

On the shore of the Wash. Large numbers of wading birds, ducks and geese, particularly as the tide is rising. ☎ 01485 542689.

Titchwell Marsh

8km (5 miles) east of Hunstanton. Wetland reed beds and shallow lagoons. Ducks, geese and, in summer, the rare marsh harrier. ☎ 01485 210779.

Strumpshaw Fen

Near to Brundall, in the heart of the Norfolk Broads. Reedbeds and woodland. Swallowtail butterflies. Many birds, including bearded tits. ☎ 01603 715191.

Surlingham Church Marsh

On the opposite side of the River Yare to Strumshaw Fen, ten kilometres (6 miles) east of Norwich. Birds of reed and sedge fen, ditches and open water. ☎ 01508 538661.

Berney Marshes and Breydon Water

Accessed from the Asda car park near Great Yarmouth railway station. Grazing marshes and mudflats. ☎ 01493 700645.

Welney Wetland Cantre

Hundred Foot Bank
Welney, Wisbech
☎ 01353 860711

tively modest size, an integral part of its environment rather than a 'foreign' intrusion as a modern industrial city might be. It is full of visitor interest and is counted among England's great heritage places as, indeed, are many of the smaller towns and villages. The main text in the appropriate chapters sings the praises of King's Lynn, Little Walsingham, Blakeney, Diss, Swaffham, East Dereham and others, whilst seaside resorts, such as Hunstanton, Sheringham, Wells-next-the-Sea and Cromer, all fulfil a different kind of holiday need.

Perhaps because of the relative scarcity of polluting industry and the wide open spaces, wildlife has always been abundant, the Fens, the Broads and the coast being particularly famous for waterfowl. This has been recognised by the creation of numerous reserves, some of national and even international importance.

In recent years, encouraged and promoted by an active tourist board, visitor attractions have increased in number, for example more farms and vineyards have opened their premises to the public, walking and cycle trails have been created, whilst Tourist Information Centres have increased their assistance to the public, including the provision of accommodation booking services in most cases.

It all adds up to an area of distinctive overall character yet, within that character, a wide diversity of landscape, of buildings and of monuments, with activities available to suit virtually any visitor.

Organisation of the Guide

This book is divided into four area chapters, loosely based on geography – North-West, North-East, South-East and South-West – roughly in accordance with the four local sheets of the Landranger Ordnance Survey maps at 1:50,000 scale. All four are of manageable size and all contain areas, towns, villages and features of visitor interest.

Indeed, the primary thrust of this Visitors Guide is its concentration on those places which visitors will enjoy, either for their inherent beauty and interest or for supplementary man-made or enhanced 'attractions' which are provided on a generous scale throughout the area. The book does not set out to be a gazetteer and the omission of a town or village means only that it is not likely to be of great interest to the majority of visitors.

Because of the considerable area covered, it has been assumed that the visitor to, say, King's Lynn or any nearby place would prefer to find his or her ancillary information (the 'FactFile') within the chapter covering just King's Lynn and its district, rather than having to wade through the much larger accumulation of similar information relating to the whole area. Consequently, the chapters are largely 'standalone', leaving the final 'FactFile' for information and issues common to all areas.

The order of the text within each chapter is 'itinerary-led'; the intention is not that the visitor will necessarily wish to follow the route of an itinerary in any slavish way but that a natural progression from place to place will be more helpful than the alternative alphabetical listing, jumping, as it must, from end to end in any particular area.

'Events' in each FactFile lists those fairs, festivals and other happenings which are of wide interest and seem to be securely established. Many of the stately homes, particularly those owned by English Heritage and the National Trust, have their own programmes, varying each year, as do the more important nature reserves.

'Places to Visit' are boxes inserted every few pages to summarise organised attractions described in the preceding text, giving opening hours and telephone numbers.

'Feature Boxes' contain a concise description of a particular feature, such as fen drainage, or of a notable person, for example, Lord Nelson.

North-West Norfolk is an interesting and varied area, lending itself well to tours and itineraries. Fringing the Fens along its western margin, the countryside soon becomes more rolling, with a long, low, chalky ridge running roughly north/south and good quality farmland prevailing. The importance of the large town of King's Lynn at the western end is balanced by the visitor potential of the more easterly coastal towns and villages such as Hunstanton, Wells-next-the-Sea and Brancaster plus the historic and present-day interest of Little Walsingham, Fakenham and East Dereham, with numerous villages, stately homes and other attractions.

The coast as a whole is among the finest in East Anglia; great swathes of sand, former tiny ports and literally mile upon mile of nature reserves.

King's Lynn

King's Lynn is a very old port and a considerable town, with charters of 1204 (King John) and later from King Henry VIII. Sir Robert Walpole, our first Prime Minister, represented King's Lynn in Parliament. The town still demonstrates its former wealth and importance, with two guildhalls, a custom house and an array of merchants' houses along the medieval streets, some of which run down to the quays on the River Great Ouse. The port is well placed for trade across the North Sea; from very early times there have been links with the Low Countries and Baltic ports, including the great Hanseatic League. Much cargo was transhipped for onward transport via the inland waterways to places such as Peterborough, Bedford and most of the Midlands.

The town hosted King John on his fateful last journey to Newark Castle,

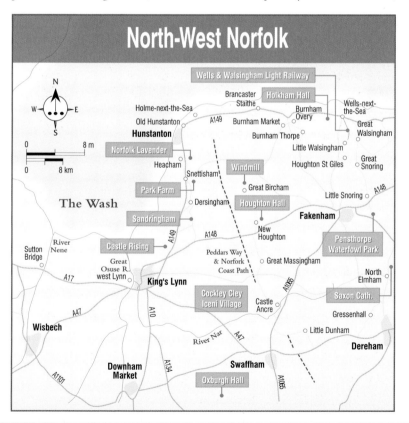

North-West Norfolk

where he died not long after arrival. More famously, his baggage train misjudged the state of the tide in the Wash and was overtaken by the swiftly rising water, with great loss; optimists are said to be still hunting for the royal valuables.

'Town Walks' leaflets are obtainable from the Tourist Information Centre. The town centre is reasonably compact, with a pedestrianised High Street linking the two marketplaces. At the north end is Tuesday Market Place, a large expanse with the old Duke's Head Hotel and the nineteenth-century Corn Exchange as the most eye-catching buildings. At the south end is the much more modest Saturday Market Place, close to St Mary's parish church, founded in 1101 as part of a Benedictine Priory. On the tower is a most unusual tidal clock. Also at Saturday Market Place is the very attractive Guildhall of the Holy Trinity comprising four parts built at different times, the oldest in 1421. This part has a magnificent facade of chequerboard flint and stone. The guildhall houses a fine collection of historic civic regalia, including the exquisite fourteenth-century 'King John's Cup'. Also part of the complex is the **Old Gaol House Museum**, a 'spine-chilling experience' of the town's former gaol, well recreated, with a personal audio tour.

Just around the corner, in Queen Street, the **Town Museum of Lynn Life** has a most evocative display of domestic life through the ages, including the earlier part of the twentieth century.

The other thoroughfare connecting the two marketplaces is King Street/Queen Street. At the north end of King Street the older Guildhall, St George's, of about 1410, is the largest remaining fifteenth-century guildhall in the country. This building has housed a wide range of activities over the centuries and is now the King's Lynn Centre for the Arts. The nearby Corn Exchange has a comprehensive programme of musical, craft fairs and similar events. The Custom House of 1683, perhaps the town's best-known building, is by the side of the street at the end of an old quay. A statue of King Charles II stands in a niche over the main doorway. A short distance further to the south, Clifton House, not open to the public, has elements from the twelfth and virtually every succeeding century, epitomising the story of the wealthy King's Lynn merchants and their houses. The notable courtyard tower is Elizabethan. Between St Mary's Church and South Quay is a former Hanseatic warehouse of 1425, now used as offices by Norfolk County Council. **Lynn Museum**, recently totally refurbished, has geological, archaeological and natural history displays, situated in a former chapel, close to Old Market Street.

A little way to the north of the town centre is the suburb of North End, where the old fishermen's quarter of tightly packed cottages housed hundreds of families close to the dominant church of St Nicholas. As the clearance of insanitary dwellings proceeded during the twentieth century, the quarter was, inevitably, demolished. Surprisingly, two cottages in True's Yard have survived and have been refurbished and furnished in period as the basis of the **True's Yard Museum**, with additional buildings providing space for historic material concerning the fishing industry.

King's Lynn has an ancient ferry, taking foot passengers at approximately 20-minute intervals across the River Great Ouse, Monday to Saturday. Modern King's Lynn has facilities consistent with a sizeable town and port, the centre of a considerable rural area – cinema, bowling arena, sports and leisure centres. From the railway station there are services direct to Cambridge and London, with connections at Ely to Peterborough (East Coast Main Line) and most parts of the Midlands.

Downham Market to Welney

Well to the south of Kings Lynn, the market town of **Downham Market**, built on rising ground, faces a great expanse of Fenland across the River Great Ouse. Notable in the Market Place is a black and white monument with clock, presented to the town in 1878. Across the river to the west of the town, a right turn from the A1122, followed in a short distance by another right turn into a minor road, leads to the remarkable **Collector's World of Eric St John Foti** at Hermitage Hall and Bridge Farm. One building has farming and other bygones and a collection of Armstrong Siddeley cars. Reconstructed Victorian streets, Dickensian Christmas, a Nelson room and much more all contribute to a truly fantastic visitor experience. The plain exteriors of the buildings give little clue to the internal interest and complexity.

To the south of Downham Market is Denver Sluice, a key feature in Fenland drainage schemes, with engineering work by the great John Rennie. The sluice separates the South Level river system from the tidal River Great Ouse and the sea. There are river moorings for pleasure craft, an inn and a car park and picnic area, with public conveniences. Close to the sluice is **Denver Windmill** of 1835 which ceased working in 1941 after the sails had been struck by lightning. The mill has been restored to full working order, with guided tours to the top of the mill. A visitor centre with craft workshop, bakery and tea room has been added.

Further to the south of Downham Market, accessed by a narrow road, is the area of fenland which includes The Washes, the land between the New and the Old Bedford Rivers. Here, the important **Welney Reserve** is operated by the Wildfowl and Wetlands Trust. A visitor centre, with tea room, is located on the edge of the Washes, with access to a considerable area of land and extensive, well-spaced, observation hides.

North of King's Lynn

The A149 leaves King's Lynn to the north as the highway serving a long section of the Norfolk coast. **Castle Rising** is soon reached. This 12-acre site has the strong and shapely keep of a Norman castle surrounded by huge earthworks, all in the care of English Heritage, who provide an audio tour. The castle was owned from 1331 to 1358 by Queen Isabella, who was involved in the murder of her husband,

King Edward II. The red brick almshouses in the adjacent village were founded in 1614 and rebuilt in 1807. There are long traditions including a special form of dress worn by the residents on ceremonial days.

Sandringham has no village, but a great 7,000-acre estate and country park owned by the Royal Family since 1862. During summer, several rooms of the great house, with surrounding grounds, an exhibition of royal cars and tea rooms are open to the public if no member of the Royal Family is in residence.

Dersingham is a large village, with a pottery/art gallery in Chapel Road. **Snettisham** has a coastal park and nature reserve reached by a long lane to Shepherd's Port, where there is provision for car parking. Coastal walks up to 4 miles (6km) in length on waymarked paths are available. To the east of the main road, Park Farm, with fun farmyard, red deer herd, adventure playground, craft workshops, tea room and gift shop, is not far from the church.

Heacham sits between the main road and the sea. In the church is an alabaster relief of the Red Indian princess, Pocahontas, who married John Rolfe of Heacham Hall whilst he was in Virginia in 1614. Unfortunately Pocahontas died at the age of 22, just three years later, leaving a son who later returned to America. Heacham Hall was destroyed by fire during World War II.

Burnham Deepdale Church

On the opposite (east) side of the main road, **Caley Mill** is prominently signposted. The mill is the centre of Norfolk Lavender, 'England's Lavender Farm', a large-scale lavender growing and marketing enterprise. The crop is picked during July and August, when visitors to the mill are offered tours of the fields and of the lavender water distillery barn at nearby Fring. A national collection of lavenders and a herb garden may also be seen. A few miles to the east, at **Great Bircham**, the fine windmill is a survivor of more than 300 such mills in Norfolk and claimed to be the only mill in working order which is open to the public. When possible the sails are used to turn the milling machinery. On site there is also a small bakery, 200 years old, with a coal-fired oven capable of baking 100 loaves at a time. The complex has cycle hire available, with advice on recommended local routes.

Hunstanton is a small, west-facing, seaside resort, with a compact shopping centre. Famous for its long cliff, rising immediately to the north of the centre, and its excellent beach, Hunstanton also has attractions such as pitch and putt and crazy golf in the clifftop gardens. Visitor facilities include the Oasis, an all-weather seafront leisure centre with swimming complex, Sea Life, with more than thirty displays, an adventure play area and the Princess Theatre. Sea tours of up to two hours' duration are available from the Central Promenade,

Admiral Lord Nelson (1758–1805)

Horatio Nelson was born at the Old Rectory, Burnham Thorpe in 1758. His father was rector of Burnham Thorpe and three of the other Burnham parishes for no less than 46 years. The Old Rectory, which was demolished in 1803, stood at the far end of the village, more than half a mile (1km) from the church; the site is marked by a roadside plaque. Inside the church Nelson's presence is felt very strongly indeed; the cross in the chancel arch and the lectern are both made from the timbers of HMS *Victory*, his flagship at the Battle of Trafalgar, where he met his death in 1805. The naval theme in the church continues with the crest of the World War II battleship *Nelson* and the flags of the World War I battle cruiser *Indomitable*. A marble bust of the great admiral is found on the wall above his father's tomb.

During the years 1787–93, when he was out of action – 'beached' – Nelson and his wife lived in Burnham Thorpe, leaving when he was offered command of the *Agamemnon*. Two years after his death, the Plough Inn was renamed the Lord Nelson. His education gives the impression of having been spread all over Norfolk, from Downham Market to Norwich and North Walsham. At Norwich, the Old Grammar School, now the school chapel, was just inside the Erpingham Gate; a marble statue of Nelson, with a telescope, is close by. At North Walsham he attended the Paston Grammar School from his tenth to his thirteenth year, leaving when his uncle was persuaded to take him on board his ship. The school still stands, on one side of the Market Square.

Those seeking out traces of Nelson will also visit the Guildhall in Norwich, where a Spanish Admiral's sword, presented by him to the city after the Battle of Cape St Vincent in 1797, is kept. On an unlikely and unattractive site in Great Yarmouth, behind the docks, a tall monument to Nelson, with the names of his four greatest battles, is crowned by the figure of Britannia.

some making use of a unique World War II DUKW amphibious vehicle.

Old Hunstanton has some attractive corners but is primarily residential, with a seafront golf course and the Le Strange Old Barns, Antiques, Arts and Crafts Centre.

At the point where the coastline turns sharply to the east, **Holme next the Sea** is a quiet village, largely bypassed by the A149. A lane leads down towards the sea, with car parking, public conveniences and refreshments at the far end. A walking track leads across the golf course to the beach, less than 400m (¼ mile) distant. Holme is notable as the northern end of the ancient Peddars Way long-distance route (see feature box).

Brancaster to Binham

Brancaster is a pleasant red-roofed village, largely strung along the main road. There is a lane to a car park, public conveniences and a spacious sandy beach. **Brancaster Staithe** ('staithe': landing place, quay), largely owned by the National Trust, is a waterside hamlet, with boating activity and a ferry (subject to the state of the tide) to Scolt Head Island, a large nature reserve.

Burnham Deepdale has a roadside church with Saxon round tower while **Burnham Market** is almost a small town, with spacious and attractive main street, inns, cafes and shops. **Burham Overy Town** is close by, but the noted Burnham Overy Mill is more than a mile (2km) distant from the village, by the side of the A149. **Burnham Overy Staithe** is another

waterside community, by the side of a sea creek, with pleasure boating centre and a ferry (tide permitting) to Scolt Head Island, with its nature reserve. In past centuries Burnham Overy Staithe was a small port but progressive silting, coupled with the arrival of the railway to this area in 1866, ended the commercial use.

Burnham Thorpe is a rather scattered village, with a large green. It is the birthplace of Horatio (later Lord) Nelson. The actual house is long gone, but a well-signposted plaque on a wall half a mile (1km) south of the village centre records the site. Inside the church, where his father was Rector for many years, there is a bust of Nelson and several relevant flags from ships of the Royal Navy. During the years of naval inactivity, 1787 to 1793, Nelson lived in the area, no doubt eager to be back in action. He was very much a Norfolk man and his memory lives on, not only in the obvious names of local inns, such as the Nelson and the Hero, but by references to be found throughout East Anglia.

The road to the south from Burnham Market soon reaches **North Creake and South Creake,** charming villages with flint-walled cottages and churches, so typical of this area. The church of Our Lady of St Mary at South Creake is particularly interesting. Despite the rigours of the Reformation, a rood screen and, more remarkably, statues including a Madonna have survived. The church is high, light and bright, with a hammer beam roof.

A mile and a quarter (2km) north of North Creake are the remains of **Creake Abbey**, in the care of English

Heritage. Originally a small hospital and almshouse for the poor, the Foundation became a Priory following the receipt of endowments. Promotion to Abbey status, of the Augustinian Order, was granted in 1231 by King Henry III. Always small in number, the Canons were decimated by plague in the early sixteenth century, only the Abbot surviving. Consequent closure in 1506 predated King Henry VIII's general Dissolution. The buildings were later used for farming purposes and as a house. The flint walling seen today is mainly of the thirteenth century, with some fifteenth-century additions.

Holkham Hall is a large stately home occupied by seven generations of the Earls of Leicester. Open to the public are a grand entrance hall, magnificent state rooms and much else, including the old kitchen. Also on site are a separate Bygones Museum, art gallery, gardens and deer park, with a sizeable lake, pottery, gift shops, tea rooms and restaurant.

The fact that **Wells–next–the–Sea** is now next to the estuary rather than the sea has not deterred Wells from carrying on as a minor port and fishing centre, with its attractive quay, narrow streets and some good Georgian houses by the green called the Buttlands. There is now a considerable presence of holiday visitors overlaying the original port activity, with a large caravan site connected to the quay by a waterside narrow-gauge railway line and a busy little market.

The town has the northern terminus of the **Wells and Walsingham Light Railway**, a narrow (10¼-inch) gauge steam-operated railway using the trackbed of the former British Rail line for 5 miles (8km) between the two named places. The journey, across rolling countryside with cuttings rich in wild flowers and butterflies, takes about half an hour. The usual locomotive is a very fine purpose-built Garratt, *Norfolk Hero* (Lord Nelson again!); open and closed coaches cater for all types of weather.

Little Walsingham is a village of enormous historical importance. Following an alleged appearance of the Blessed Virgin in a dream to Richeldis, Lady of the Manor of Walsingham, a shrine was established by Richeldis as a replica of the Holy House in Nazareth where the angel Gabriel announced to Mary that she was to be the Mother of God. The shrine soon became the most important Marian shrine in Christendom, a place of pilgrimage until it was destroyed on the instructions of King Henry VIII following his break with the Roman Catholic Church. The religious history throughout the succeeding centuries has involved both Roman Catholics and Anglicans, with the recommencement of pilgrimage in 1897.

The most appropriate route for a visit to Little Walsingham starts at the 'Slipper Chapel' near Houghton St Giles, where the fourteenth-century chapel has been supplemented by modern buildings, forming the National Roman Catholic Shrine of Our Lady. At this chapel, medieval pilgrims would shed their shoes to walk barefoot for the last mile to the shrine. On entering Little Walsingham the ruin of the Friary (no public access) is seen to the left. At the far end of High Street the ruins of the Abbey, founded in 1153 by Augustinian canons, are to the right. The entrance is through the Tourist Information Centre, round the corner in Common Place. Finally, a little further to the right, in Holt Road, is the modern (1931) Anglican Shrine, claiming to be 'England's Nazareth', beautifully set in gardens, with accommodation for pilgrims adjacent. To complete the overwhelming religious presence, there is also an impressive parish church, the only Georgian Methodist chapel (of 1794) still in use in East Anglia and a Russian Orthodox Chapel in the former railway station.

With or without an interest in religious history, Little Walsingham is an attractive place for visitors, with timber-framed buildings and Georgian facades. The modern visitor need not be any type of pilgrim to enjoy the inns, restaurants and tea rooms which serve the village.

The southern terminus of the Wells and Walsingham Light Railway is close to the village centre. For guided tours of Little Walsingham, apply at the Tourist Information Centre (Tel. 01328 850510).

By contrast with its 'Little' namesake, **Great Walsingham** is quite an ordinary sort of place, pleasant but without distinction. The parish church of St Peter is a good example of an unspoilt church of the Decorated period. The Great Walsingham Barns, housed in converted Norfolk farm buildings with a lovely courtyard, has paintings, sculpture and textiles. Apart from the names, the charm of **Great Snoring and Little Snoring** lies in the flint cottages and a village sign which commemorates years of local Royal Air Force activity.

Binham has a Benedictine Priory founded in 1091. Always poor in comparison with most other monastic houses, Binham was dissolved in 1540. Now used as a parish church and for musical events throughout the summer, the surviving building has a magnificent west front with an Early English arch, rare in East Anglia. The ruins of the other Priory buildings are adjacent.

Thursford to Houghton

Thursford is known for its 'Collection', an extravaganza of restored road and agricultural steam engines and fairground organs, with catering, specialised shops and daily performances on a Wurlitzer organ, all accommodated in an attractive complex. Between Thurlford and Fakenham, the Old Barn Studios at **Kettlestone** have fine art, with specialisation in bird and plant life, visiting artists for special exhibitions and painting and drawing courses during the summer. **Fakenham** is one of north Norfolk's largest market towns and a road communication centre for the area. The shopping centre, with supermarkets both in and out of town, is hugely complemented by the Thursday market which, coupled with the concurrent auction sale, covers much of the town centre. Architecturally, the town centre is largely eighteenth century; it is well provided with inns and restaurants. National Hunt meetings are held at the reacecourse on the edge of town, which has sufficient space to accommodate a large caravan site.

The **Museum of Gas and Local History** is sited at the town's redundant gasworks, now a scheduled ancient monument. The museum has recently been refurbished. There is a golf course by the racecourse and a golf driving range with pitch and putt a little way out of town on the Burnham Market Road. About 2 miles (3km) along the Norwich road, the A1067, **Pensthorpe Water Park and Nature Reserve** claims to have the largest collection of waterfowl in Europe. The present visitor centre buildings were opened by the Duke of Edinburgh in 1988. The centre is very attractive, with audio-visual display, special exhibitions and a luxurious viewing gallery. Some of the more unusual birds such as scarlet ibis, spoonbills and little egrets, are kept in enclosures, but the majority are unconfined, seen on or around the series of lakes created from former gravel workings, now beautifully landscaped. Waymarked trails with a suggested walking time of up to two hours thread their way through the extensive grounds. Buggies are provided for those who need them.

North Elmham, between Fakenham and East Dereham, has the site of a former Saxon cathedral, a timber building which was the seat of the Bishop of East Anglia until 1071, when he moved to Thetford and, later, to Norwich. The cathedral became a parish church until about 1100, when it was replaced by a stone chapel for the private use of Bishop Herbert of Norwich. During the latter part of the fourteenth century it was converted to a castle for a later Bishop of Norwich. It fell into disuse in the sixteenth century and is now nothing more than a substantial ruin.

Gressenhall, close to East Dereham, has the **Norfolk Rural Life Museum** occupying a substantial former workhouse. A wide-ranging collection of farming bygones, with reconstructed shops and workplaces displaying how people have lived and worked in Norfolk during the past 150 years or so, comprises a major visitor attraction. The museum has ramps rather than steps, wheelchair loan and disabled facilities, gift shop and tea room. The adjacent Union Farm, operated in conjunction with the museum, is stocked with rare breeds of cattle, sheep and pigs. There are woodland walks and a riverside trail.

East Dereham is one of the bigger agricultural centres and market towns of Norfolk. In fact there are two market days, large on Friday and small on Tuesday, complementing the generally good shopping facilities. Most of the town's buildings are later than the second of two great fires of the sixteenth and seventeenth centuries; understandably, eighteenth-century facades now dominate. The poet William Cowper, who died in 1800, is buried in the churchyard, with a window and a monument to his memory. Bishop Bonner's Cottages of 1502 are named after a sixteenth-century rector who went on to become Bishop of London. The cottages, of brick, flint, wattle and daub construction, have ornamental plasterwork. An archaeological museum now occupies the cottages. **Dereham Mill**, in Cherry Lane, just off the Norwich road, was built in 1836 as a brick tower corn mill with four sails and the usual fantail. The sails were removed in 1922, the stones being driven by an external paraffin engine. Production finally ceased in 1937. Following several years of decay the building was purchased in 1979 by Breckland District Council and, over a period of eight years, the mill was restored as a landscape feature, but not to full working order. **Dereham Station** is the headquarters of the volunteer group engaged in restoring a considerable length of the former Mid-Norfolk Railway line. So far, about 11 miles (18km) of the line between Dereham and Wymondham is back in use and there are ambitious plans to restore more of the track towards Fakenham.

The villages of **Little Dunham** and **Litcham** each have a museum. That at Dunham has a collection of old working tools, bygones and machinery, and a dairy, leathersmith and shoemaker. Litcham Village Museum has artefacts from Roman times onwards, an underground lime kiln and a photographic collection.

Swaffham is another attractive market town, compact, busy and a centre for a rural hinterland. There are plenty of shops, inns and cafés. The town clusters around the wedge-shaped Market Square, which has a notable domed and pillared butter cross. The statue on the top is of Ceres, goddess of agriculture. Also in the Market Square is the elegant former Assembly Room of 1817. The church of St Peter and St Paul was renewed in the fifteenth century, with a sixteenth-century tower and a newer delicate spire with a copper ball. Inside, the double hammer beam roof has 150 angels and richly moulded timbers. The well-known Swaffham legend concerns a fifteenth-century local pedlar by the name of John Chapman who had a dream that if he went to London and stood on London Bridge he would become a wealthy man. He did this and, sure enough, after a few days a shopkeeper accosted him and was told the story set out in Chapman's dream. By an amazing coincidence the shopkeeper had himself had a dream that in Swaffham a pot of gold had been buried in a pedlar's garden. Chapman hurried back home and, digging in his garden, found not one, but two pots of gold. He gave the church a large proportion of the cash, used to rebuild the north aisle. It has to be said that Chapman's story is by no means universally accepted.

Swaffham Museum is in the town hall, London Street, an eighteenth-century building formerly the house of a brewer. The museum has local history, temporary exhibitions and displays on prominent local figures such as W.E. Johns, the creator of Biggles. The **EcoTech Centre** is an exciting modern environmental attraction with an innovative 'green' building, imaginative exhibitions, interactive displays, many of which fascinate children, and a café.

Castle Acre is a very attractive and historic village with a wealth of visitor interest, strategically sited at the point where the ancient Peddars Way crosses the River Nar. William de Warenne, son-in-law of William the Conqueror, constructed a great motte (mound) crowned by a powerful flint keep. Most of the present village lies within what was the outer bailey of this castle. Pass the huge church of St James to visit the remains of the great eleventh-century **Castle Acre Priory**, founded by the Cluniac Order and now owned

The Peddars Way

The Peddars Way is a very old route, certainly used by the Romans, but also very likely to pre-date the Roman conquest as a 'war road' of the Iceni tribe or as more mundane salt tracks. The Roman road was built immediately after AD 61, following the great revolt of Boudicca and her Iceni tribesmen, for the purpose of facilitating rapid troop movements, vital for keeping the tribesmen under control. The generally straight alignment and the very substantial dimensions of the construction – up to 45ft (13.7m) in width and 2ft 6in (760mm) thickness of the embankment (agger) in places – confirm the military purpose.

The length traced is from Holme next the Sea on the Norfolk coast to just south of Coney Weston in Suffolk, about 50 miles (80km), almost certainly linking with a ferry across the Wash at the north end. This gave a through route to Burgh in the Marsh, Lincolnshire, and thence to the Roman garrison at Lincoln. There is a known Roman road between those places. After the Roman departure, the Saxons had no real use for what was, to them, a rather mysterious historic highway leading to and from places beyond their experience. Consequently their villages were built away from the line of the road.

Today, the Way comprises country lanes, waymarked bridleways and footpaths. It is all available to walkers and much of the distance is also used by horse riders. At Holme next the Sea there is a link with the Norfolk Coast Path to provide a continuous National Trail of 93 miles (150km). Despite the lack of villages apart from Castle Acre and West Acre, there are interesting features along the Way. Swaffham, Great Bircham, Great and Little Massingham and Ringstead are not far from the direct line. Anmer Minque and Bircham Heath have round barrow burial mounds. The re-creation of an Iceni village at Cockley Cley is likewise accessible. The countryside ranges from the heath of Breckland via the north-west Norfolk ridge to the dunes of the coast.

There is a good deal of accommodation along the route and circular walks are being developed at several places, based on the Peddars Way. Appropriate booklets will be published. Particular efforts will be made to ensure access to these routes by public transport.

by English Heritage. There is an informative visitor centre and, on the site proper, a glorious west front, decorated arches and interesting and varied use of building materials, including flint, brick and two varieties of limestone – Caen and Barnack. The grounds of the Priory make a splendid venue for a summer programme of open air events, including 'medieval' fairs and entertainment. Close by is **West Acre**, where the ruins of the Priory are not open to the public and are not easily seen from the public road. **West Acre Gardens** are situated just over a mile (2km) from the village.

A plant lover's paradise, the gardens offer many unusual species.

Great Massingham has one of the largest village greens in Norfolk, divided by minor roadways and studded with ponds, some of them virtually lakes. Flint-built houses and the church of St Mary complete a lovely scene. Inside the church, the front of the high altar glows with the gold leaf finish on an intricate woodcarving of 1953.

Houghton Hall is a grand Palladian house built in the 1720s for Sir Robert Walpole, our first prime minister. James Gibbs was one of the architects and

EcoTech Centre, Swaffham

the interiors are by William Kent. It is privately owned and is the seat of the Marquess of Cholmondeley. Open to the public are parts of the house, a walled garden, parkland with a large herd of white fallow deer, tea room and gift shop. A specialised museum has the Cholmondeley collection of model soldiers, 20,000 of them, deployed in the representation of famous battles.

Walks

In addition to the greater part of the Peddars Way, this part of Norfolk also includes the Nar Valley Way, a route following the course of the River Nar for 34 miles (54km) from King's Lynn to the Norfolk Museum of Rural Life at Gressingham, near East Dereham, passing through West Acre and Castle Acre on the way. The route follows public rights of way, tracks and minor roads, with plenty of intermediate car parking provision. Overnight accommodation is available at Castle Acre, about halfway along the route.

Here are just a few suggestions from the many short walks typical of this area.

1. Great Massingham

From Little Massingham, a short distance north of Great Massingham, drive along a very minor road past the church. After about three quarters of a mile (1km) park at a grassy triangle a little way past a road junction. Walk on for a few yards to a broad, unsurfaced lane and turn left. This lane is part of the famous Peddars Way; there are waymarks on a post. The Way rises very gently, almost but not quite straight, an ancient track beside fields of corn. In about two thirds of a mile (just under 1km) turn left at a junction; there is a waymarked post. The new track is similar to the Peddars Way, heading for communications masts and Great Massingham. Close to the masts, the track becomes a concrete roadway, bordered by cornfields. Ox-eye daisies, field edge poppies and bindweed add a little colour.

The edge of Great Massingham soon comes into view. Join a minor public road (if time is pressing there is a sharp left turn along a surfaced lane here which will bring you back to the parking place in not much more than two thirds of a mile (1km)). However, it would be a shame not to continue into Great Massingham. Turn right along the public road, soon reaching the northern edge of the largest of the several village ponds. To explore the spacious and attractive village turn right towards the church, the Rose and Crown Inn and the post office/village stores. The best return route is to retrace your steps along the minor road, passing the point at which our track joined, and then bear right; this is the lane recommended above as a short cut. The overall distance, including exploring Great Massingham, is about 3 miles (5km).

A little longer and much more adventurous return can be made by using footpaths which start to the north of the village. Turn left off the Little Massingham road, into Sunnyside, then through a gate. The path is rather vague. Continue to a junction of paths, through more gates and close to a fence on the left. The path continues in a fairly straight line along the edge of a cultivated field, becoming more overgrown until eventually a way has to be forced through the undergrowth by a tree belt to reach a cornfield. Go across or round the right-hand edge of the field to a strip of trees on the far side, where there is a good path among the trees. Turn right to walk to a minor road, where there is a farm almost opposite. Turn left to return to the parking place in less than a quarter of a mile (0.5km).

2. Castle Acre

Park in the village centre and walk on along Priory Road, with the large church on the left. At a T-junction turn left by the public conveniences if visiting the Priory. Otherwise, turn right at the junction, then left in 65 yeards (60m). At a 'Nar Valley Way' signpost go along a stony surfaced lane. After a right-hand bend turn left in approximately 200yds/200m through a waymarked kissing gate. A good grassy path keeps close to the modest River Nar for some distance until the woodland of the West Acre Estate is entered at another kissing gate. Squirrels and pheasants may be seen here.

Leave the wood at an old iron gate to cross a rough meadow. Go over a stream on a wooden footbridge. The large house to the left is Mill House. Cross another footbridge over the River Nar to reach a public road. Turn right towards a ford and footbridge, but turn left immediately before the bridge to follow a clear footpath, at first quite close to the river. The way is clear; as the tracks divide keep to the wider. Join a more important track, turning sharp left, then right in a further 10 yards (10m). (To visit West Acre village, turn right along the more important track and cross the river by the footbridge).

After the right turn follow a waymarked path along the edge of a field. Go straight across the public road to a broad, sandy, agricultural track with signpost, slightly uphill. Pass the end of a tree belt, still rising. As the track bends sharply to the right, turn left along a waymarked 'road used as public path' along the bottom edge of a field, now almost level. Go straight across a junction. The fields have crops of sugar beet, with some wheat, enlivened by the colour of field edge poppies and ox-eye daisies, with busy butterflies. Turn left at the next junction to pass an isolated house before reaching a large farm complex. As a wide driveway sweeps to the right into the farm, go straight on here to join the road. Turn right for about quarter of a mile (400m); over a gate on the left of the road part of an ancient moat can be seen. Pass the flint church of St George, South Acre. Fork left at 'Ford – unsuitable for motors', then left again to pass a house called 'Little Brooms'. Continue along an unsurfaced lane, with glimpses of the ruin of Castle Acre Priory. Cross the river by the footbridge at a pretty spot, then rise along the surfaced road towards Castle Acre village. Reach the church, then turn right, back to the village centre. Without diversion, about 6¼ miles (10km) in length.

3. Burnham Thorpe

Park vehicles on the grassy area in front of the church. Walk away from the church to the right along a minor surfaced road. As the road bends to the right, strike off left up a broad rising stony track, with a little woodland to the left. There is a good view of the well-known church below. Cross a minor public road and continue along a broad, almost straight, track between hedges towards Lucas Hill Wood, in Holkham Park. In about half a mile (1km) turn right by a substantial flint and tile agricultural building to take

an obvious track with a hedge on the right, rising gently to pass an active air landing strip, with an appropriate warning notice.

The route now bends to the right, gently downhill. Cross a minor road and continue as before, now between hedgerows, soon reaching another public road. Turn left to cross the tiny River Burn immediately before a road junction. Turn right; in 100m the signposted plaque recording Nelson's birthplace is seen on the left. Return to the junction and continue towards Fakenham for 100m. Turn right into another broad lane, rising gently, soon passing a large stone and brick disused farm building then reaching a more important public road (B1355). Turn right to follow the road uphill for just over half a mile (almost 1km). Near the crest turn right into a broad stony track, slightly uphill.

At the top of Gravelpit Hill there is a small wood on the right. Although the hill is only 132ft (40m) high, by Norfolk standards this is quite a commanding position, with an extensive panorama. Below is Burnham Thorpe village, whilst the sea can be seen to the left, beyond Burnham Overy Staithe. The track descends to a minor road. Go straight across, pass a farm on the right, and reach another road in 100m. Turn left briefly and then right, to follow the little road round to the church. The main part of the village is to the right.

Cycle Rides

North-West Norfolk is a splendid area for cyclists. There are no great hills but most of the countryside is sufficiently undulating to give the interest of frequently changing views over farming land, well dotted with towns and villages. There is also the coastal strip with some of its nature reserves readily reached on two wheels. The 'Norfolk Coast Cycleway' from King's Lynn to Cromer is the subject of a leaflet obtainable at relevant tourist information centres. A map-guide with full detail is available from the tourist information centre at Cromer. Most of this area is well provided with minor roads, quiet lanes for the most part, very suitable for cycling. Many of the visitor attractions which could provide the destination for a day out are well away from major centres of population and the attendant busy roads.

The Wensum Valley and adjacent area has well-organised routes throughout its length, from close to Norwich to Raynham and Rudham villages. Excellent leaflets at very small cost include the actual routes, places of interest, suggestions for accommodation and useful addresses and telephone numbers.

Cycle hire and walks for all the family are offered at Great Bircham Mill (Tel. 01485 578393).

Car Tours

Most motorists will no doubt want to give emphasis to destinations along the coast. Without leaving the area covered by this chapter, the A149 provides the connection between King's Lynn, Castle Rising, Sandringham, Hunstanton, Brancaster, Burnham Market and Wells-next-the-Sea. The obvious return for a circular excursion is via Fakenham using the A148. Add the odd stately home or windmill and there is

more than enough for several days out. To continue along the coast to Blakeney, Sheringham and Cromer, returning inland by Felbrigg, Blickling and Aylsham, is still well within reach.

Norwich is almost an obligatory destination from bases in all the areas covered by chapters in this book. A visit to the city can readily be combined with the Norfolk Broads but there is so much of interest for whole families that it really does merit a day to itself. Its features are set out in Chapter 3. For a different kind of experience, particularly recommended for young families, an excursion to Great Yarmouth for sand, pier and pleasure beach is a good day out, possibly combining the trip with some part of the Norfolk Broads en route.

Inland destinations, ranging from Stamford, Spalding and Boston in the southern part of Lincolnshire to Peterborough (Nene Valley Railway), Ely and Cambridge are all worthy of consideration.

Public Transport

Railway services are restricted to the line which runs from London, Cambridge and Ely to King's Lynn, the 'Fen Line', most of which is outside the scope of this book. The service to London is generally hourly. Bus services cover the principal towns and many villages and there are specialised services such as the 'Coasthopper' between Hunstanton and Sheringham. There is also a 'Hop On, Hop Off' service along the route of the Peddars Way.

For information on all bus services in Norfolk, call Traveline – Tel. 0870 608 2 608.

Places to Visit

King's Lynn

Old Gaol House Museum and Civic Regalia *W*

Trinity Guildhall
☎ 01553 774297
Open Apr to end of Oct, Mon to Sat 10am–5pm; Nov to Mar, Tue to Sat 10am–4pm.

True's Yard Museum *W*

North Street
☎ 01553 765100
Tea room with light refreshments all day
Open all year except Christmas Day from 9.30am, last admissions 3.45pm.

Lynn Museum *W*

Market Street
☎ 01553 775001
Open all year, Tue to Sat 10am–5pm. Closed on public holidays. Admission free.

Town House Museum of Lynn Life *W*

Queen Street
☎ 01553 773450
Open May to Sep, Mon to Sat 10am–5pm; Oct to Apr, Mon to Sat 10am–4pm. Closed on bank holidays.

The Green Quay (Wash Discovery Centre) *W*

Marriot's Warehouse, South Quay
☎ 01553 818500
Open daily, 9am–5pm. Admission free.

The Custom House

Purfleet Quay
☎ 01553 763044
The Tourist Information Centre is situated on the ground floor. Guided walks are available from May to Oct
Open Apr to Sep, Mon to Sat 10am–4.30pm, Sun 12–4.30pm; Oct to Mar, Mon to Sat 10.30am–3.30pm, Sun 12–3.30pm.

Pensthorpe Waterfowl Park

Norfolk Arena   W

Saddlebow Road
☎ 01553 771111
Speedway, banger racing and related events.

Strikes Bowling Arena   W

1–5 Lynn Road, Gaywood
☎ 01553 760333
Open 10.00 until late, every day.

Caithness Glass   W

Paxman Road, Hardwick Industrial Estate
☎ 01553 765111
Glassmaking centre and factory shop
Open 7 days a week, Mar to Christmas, 6 days during the rest of the year. Glassmaking Mon to Fri.

King's Lynn Sports and Leisure Centre   W

Green Park Avenue
☎ 01553 818001.

Downham Market to Welney

Collectors' World of Eric St John Foti   W

☎ 01366 383185
Open daily all year, 11am to 5pm (last entry 4pm).

Denver Windmill   W

☎ 01366 384009
Visitor centre, guided tours, café, bakery and shop
Open Apr to Oct, Mon to Sat 10am–5pm, Sun 12–5pm; Nov to Mar, Mon to Sat 10am–4pm, Sun 12–4pm.

Welney Nature Reserve

The Washes
☎ 01353 860711.

Castle Rising to Holme

Castle Rising

☎ 01553 631330
Open from beginning of Apr to end of Oct, daily 10am–6pm (or dusk in Oct); Nov to end of Mar, Wed to Sun 10am–4pm. Closed 24–26 Dec.

Sandringham   W

☎ 01553 612908
The Norfolk retreat of Her Majesty The Queen
Visitor centre with shop and café open all the year round (closed Mons and Tues in winter). House, car museum and gardens open from mid-Apr to end Oct, 10.30am–5pm.

Dersingham Pottery   W

Open daily all year, 10am–5.30pm

Park Farm

Snettisham
☎ 01485 542425
Gift shop and tea room
Open daily from 10am–5pm (telephone for winter opening hours).

Norfolk Lavender

Heacham
☎ 01485 570384
Plant centre, gift shop and tea room
Open Apr to Oct 9.30am–5pm; Nov to Mar 9.30am–4pm. Guided tours, Spring Bank Holiday to end of Sep, several times daily.

Old Barns Antiques, Arts and Crafts Centre   W

Old Hunstanton
☎ 01485 533402
Open daily, 10am–5pm

Great Bircham Windmill   W

☎ 01485 578393
Gift shop, tea rooms, bakery and cycle hire. Open daily from Easter to the end of Sep, 10am–5pm.

Places to Visit

Oasis   W
Hunstanton
☎ 01485 534227
Open from early Feb to late Nov. Telephone for public access times to pools.

Sea Life   W
Hunstanton
☎ 01485 533576
Café and gift shop
Open daily from 10am in summer. Check for winter opening times.

Princess Theatre   W
Hunstanton
☎ 01485 532252.

Searles' Sea Tours
☎ 01485 534444
Includes occasional use of a World War II DUKW.

Brancaster to Binham

Holkham Hall   W
☎ 01328 710227
Stately Home, Bygones museum, art gallery, gift shops, tea rooms, restaurant, nursery gardens
Open (house) Easter, May to the end of Sep, Suns to Thus 12–5pm. The Nursery Gardens are open every day except Christmas and Boxing Days, 10am–5pm (or dusk if earlier). Opening of the stables restaurant and the pottery shop is generally similar to the house but includes Fris, extends through Oct, and commences each day at 10am. The separate Bygones Museum is open from late May to Sep, Sun to Thu (☎ 01328 713112).

Wells and Walsingham Light Railway   W
☎ 01328 711630
Open daily from Apr to the end of Oct.

Shirehall (Courthouse) Museum   W
Little Walsingham (adjoining the Tourist Information Centre) ☎ 01328 820510
Open from Easter to the end of Oct, Mon to Sat 10am–4.30pm. Weekends only out of season.

Walsingham Abbey Grounds
☎ 01328 820510 or 820259
Open all year. Entrance in summer months through Shirehall Museum and Tourist Information Centre (☎ 01328 820510); out of season, entrance through adjacent estate office (☎ 01328 820259).

Great Walsingham Barns   W
Gallery and shops. Textile Centre.
Open daily 10am–5pm.

Binham Priory   W (church only)
Open at all reasonable times.

Thursford to Houghton

EcoTech Centre   W
☎ 01760 726100
Turbine Way, Swaffham
Sustainable environmental education.

Thursford Collection   W
☎ 01328 878477
Tea rooms. Open Good Fri to late Oct, 12–5pm.

Fakenham Museum of Gas and Local History   W
Hempton Road
☎ 01328 863150
Open early Aug to mid-Sep, Thus and Bank Holidays, 10.30am–3.30pm.

Fakenham Driving Range and Pitch and Putt course
Burnham Market Road
☎ 01328 856614
Open daily 10am–10pm.

Pensthorpe Waterfowl Park and Nature Reserve

☎ 01328 851465
Restaurant, countryside shop, adventure play area
Open daily 10am–5pm.

Norfolk Rural Life Museum and Union Farm   *W*

Gressenhall
☎ 01362 860563
Tea room, facilities for disabled visitors
Open from early Apr to the beginning of Nov, 10am–5pm.

Dereham Windmill

Cherry Lane, Dereham
Under renovation. Enquire at TIC
(☎ 01362 698992).

Dereham Station

☎ 01362 690633
Headquarters of the preserved Mid-Norfolk Railway, 11 miles (18km) from Dereham to Wymondham. Souvenir shop, refreshments and toilets
Open when services are running; telephone for up to date information.

Swaffham Museum   *W*

☎ 01760 721230 for opening hours.

Anglian Karting Centre

The Airfield, North Pickenham
☎ 01760 441777
Open from the beginning of Apr to the end of Sep, Wed 2–9pm, Sat 1–6pm, Sun 12.30–6pm, Bank Holidays 10.30am–6pm. Also open most weekends in winter, Sat 1–5pm, Sun 12.30–5pm.

Litcham Village Museum   *W*

'Fourways', Litcham
☎ 01328 701383
Open from early Apr to early Oct, Sats and Suns 2–5pm.

Dunham Museum

Little Dunham
Open all year, Suns 10am–5pm.

Castle Acre Priory

(English Heritage)
☎ 01760 755394
Open Jan to late Mar, Wed to Sun 10am–4pm; late Mar to the end of Oct, daily 10am–1pm and 2–6pm (or dusk in Oct); Nov and Dec, Wed to Sun 10am–4pm. Closed 24 to 26 Dec.

West Acre Gardens

Open daily, Feb to Nov, 10am–5pm

Houghton Hall   *W*

near King's Lynn
☎ 01485 528569
House open from Easter to the end of Sep, Suns, Weds, Thus and Bank Holiday Mons, 1.30–5.30pm. (House). Tea room, shop, gardens and other facilities open from 11am.

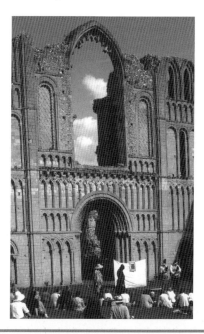

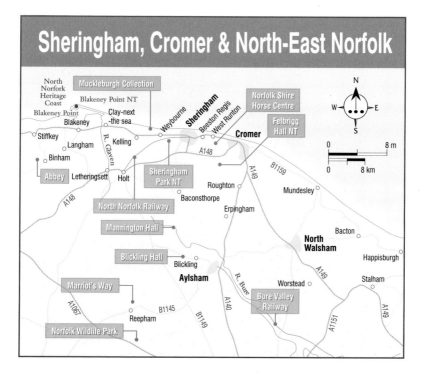

North-east Norfolk is deservedly a popular holiday area, with its fine coastline backed in many places by low cliffs and with higher ground inland, including Norfolk's highest point at Beacon Hill. The Victorian holiday resorts of Sheringham and Cromer have retained much of their popularity. Quite different is the coast at Blakeney and Cley next the Sea. The attraction here is of an altogether quieter nature, with both fresh and salt marshes and the seal colonies at Blakeney Point.

Sheringham, Cromer & North-East Norfolk

Much of the coast has been designated as an Area of Outstanding Natural Beauty. Inland the towns, largely set in rolling countryside, are varied and attractive, with evidence of the historical importance of the wool trade at places such as Worstead. Major visitor centres, including the National Trust stately homes at Blickling and Felbrigg, add to the overall interest of this area. The itinerary-based information set out below starts and finishes at the coast.

Sheringham is a nineteenth-century seaside resort, largely of Victorian and Edwardian buildings, founded on a historic fishing village. The seafaring tradition is now mainly evidenced by the manning of the lifeboat. The clean-washed sandy beach is a great attraction, supplemented by a leisure pool, museum and various other visitor facilities. The Little Theatre opens from May to September, with a programme which includes films and theatrical productions. The **Sheringham Museum** is located in a converted fishermen's cottage in Station Road. Displays include the fishing and holiday industries and boat building. There is also a **Fishermen's Heritage Centre** at West Cliff.

The **North Norfolk Railway** is a mainly steam-operated preserved line, using the trackbed of part of the former British Rail branch between Sheringham and Holt, with an intermediate stop at Weybourne. Originally this line was part of the Midland and Great Northern Joint Railway. At Sheringham, the station area has static exhibits, shop and buffet. Rather more unusually, tuition in driving a steam locomotive is on offer. The line winds around the

end of the wooded hill behind the town and is scenically attractive. There is a service, much reduced out of season, during each month other than January. Two former 'Brighton Belle' Pullman restaurant coaches are used for serving special meals.

Sheringham has plentiful shopping facilities, busy roads and streets and, arguably, more than enough informal catering. There is a railway, the 'Bittern Line', with an approximately hourly service to and from Norwich and the town is on the Norfolk Coasthopper bus route.

Behind Sheringham is a ridge of wooded land, high by East Anglian standards, where Upper Sheringham is a separate residential area. **Sheringham Park**, designed in 1812 by Humphry Repton, the great landscape gardener, is now owned by the National Trust. From the park there are spectacular

Muckleborough Collection at Weybourne

views of coast and countryside, magnificent rhododendrons, viewing towers and walks. Very occasionally, at some Bank Holidays, a restored 1920s steam-powered sawmill is operated. 'Pretty Corner' has a car park.

At Beeston Regis, on the eastern edge of Sheringham, **Priory Maze** has an attractive wild flower meadow, ponds, stream and wildlife all adding to the attraction of the maze itself. Just beyond Weybourne, the **Muckleburgh Collection** claims to be Britain's largest working military collection, privately owned and all under cover. Tank demonstrations are given on Sundays and Bank Holiday Mondays, and also on weekdays during school summer holidays.

West Runton is soon reached, where the **Norfolk Shire Horse Centre** has also the Countryside Collection of farming bygones and a Children's Farm. Working demonstrations of such crafts as harnessing are given and there are cart rides for children, a video show and an indoor area for wet weather demonstrations. There is a riding school adjacent to the centre.

Cromer is the other traditional seaside holiday resort of the north Norfolk Coast, long famous for its sea fishing, with crabs as the speciality. Like all good seaside resorts, the popularity of Cromer is founded on its fine beach, supplemented by the visitor attractions such as the **pier** with its **theatre**, which has a programme of summer shows, and the **museum**, housed in a row of tiny fishermen's cottages beside the church, exhibiting much local material and a reconstituted Victorian fisherman's cottage. There is also the RNLI Henry

Blogg **lifeboat museum**. In addition to the profusion of shops, cafés and restaurants, Cromer does have a small old town, with narrow streets pressing close to the church of St Peter and St Paul. The church tower, at 160ft (49m), is the highest in Norfolk. The town is served by the Bittern Line railway to Sheringham and Norwich and by the Coasthopper bus service. Behind Cromer two designated footpaths, the Norfolk Coast Path and The Weavers' Way (see feature boxes), join together.

A short diversion inland, close to Roughton, the National Trust owned Jacobean mansion of **Felbrigg** has been growing gradually over more than three centuries. Four generations of the Windham family and their successors have accumulated furniture, books and pictures to fill its beautiful rooms. 'Grand tour' paintings and ornate plasterwork are particular features. A walled garden of almost 3 acres (1 hectare), with octagonal dovecote, is the highlight of the gardens, which are surrounded by a spacious park, largely wooded, and with several designated trails. Facilities include the Park Restaurant, the Turret Tea Room, picnic area, shop and bookshop. All ground floor facilities are accessible to wheelchair users; wheelchairs are freely available.

Mundesley, North Walsham and Reepham

The next stop heading east along the coast is **Mundesley**, an altogether different sort of place, quiet and discreet, a former fishing hamlet catering for much

smaller numbers of visitors. The hamlet has a modern overlay, with an excellent sandy beach backed by floral decorations and a mini-golf course. Also close to the beach is a much restored church and a tiny Maritime Museum, operated on a voluntary basis. A little way inland is a useful range of shops.

After Mundesley a long stretch of the coastline is relatively undistinguished, with a large oil terminal close to Bacton. **Happisburgh** has good access to the sea, with a safe bathing beach. The fifteenth-century church, with its tower visible from well out to sea, and also a lighthouse, both contribute as aids to navigation. Turning inland for a few kilometres, **North Walsham** is a pleasant small market town, with a distinctive market cross of 1549, subsequently damaged and restored. Nelson attended Paston Grammar School for three years. The school is still here, but has been rebuilt since Nelson's day. The large parish church of St. Nicholas, mainly fourteenth-century, has the dubious distinction of a ruined tower. There is an elaborate porch with statues; inside

are fine arcades, a massively ornamental font cover, an impressive organ and much more.

The town has plenty of individual shops and, much more unusually, a Conservation Award-winning Woolworth's store in a converted inn. The **Motor Cycle Museum**, close to the railway station, has more than 60 motorcycles dating from the 1920s to the 1960s. There is a railway service to and from Norwich, Cromer and Sheringham on the Bittern Line. Thursday is market day.

Worstead may be small but it is certainly significant, having given its name to a finely woven cloth well known throughout Britain for centuries. The industry was founded by immigrant Flemish weavers in Norman times and their lasting monument is the great church which they erected in the fourteenth century, truly a 'wool church'. The large nave has a hammer beam roof, great screens and a fine font cover. In Church Plain, close by, there are several seventeenth-century weavers' houses.

The **Dinosaur Adventure Park** is close to the A1067 at Lenwade, south of Reepham, some 12 miles (20km) west across country from Worstead. Here, one of the world's largest collections of life-size replicas of dinosaurs can be seen, spread throughout acres of woodland. The models are complemented by an adventure play area, crazy golf, refreshments and a picnic area. About 3 miles (5km) further west along the main road, **The Animal Ark** (formerly the Norfolk Wildlife Park) at Great Witchingham has a good array of animals, for the most part housed in quite spacious paddocks in 40 acres of parkland. Included are reindeer, lynx, barbary apes and birds of prey, with the emphasis on native species, and also a model farm, with rare domestic breeds of farm animal. Visitor facilities comprise a tea room and terrace, gift shop and children's play area.

Reepham is one of the smaller towns of the area, now less important than it was in the eighteenth century, when it had a market and was the centre of a barley-growing and brewing district. The old marketplace has some attractive buildings, including the Kings Arms Inn, with a notably Dutch/Flemish influence apparent. The churchyard once had no fewer than three churches within its compass. One has been a ruin since 1543, only a fragment now remaining, but St Michael's, the church of neighbouring Whitwell parish, still stands back to back with St Mary's, the parish church of Reepham, a curious arrangement. The latter church has an unusual Norman font. At the former Reepham Station there is a small museum, tea room and gift shop. Twenty-one miles (34km) of the trackbed of former railway lines have been made available as a rural trail for walkers, cyclists and horse riders. This route has been designated 'Marriott's Way' in memory of William Marriott, chief engineer of the former Midland and Great Northern Joint Railway for 41 years. The Way is made up of parts of that railway and the Great Eastern Railway. There is a link with the Riv-

Cromer

erside Path at the Norwich end of the line, increasing the length of the route by a further 5 miles (8km). For walkers there is also a link with the 'Weavers' Way' long-distance footpath and with the Bure Valley Walk at Aylsham (see 'walks' below).

From Aylsham to Cley

Aylsham is a small market town with well-varied architecture and many individual shops around its largely red brick Market Place. Until the Industrial Revolution, the town was a considerable wool centre. The Millgate area was formerly a small port on the River Bure, trading with Norwich and Great Yarmouth, but flooding and the arrival of the railways put an end to this trade and the eighteenth-century buildings are now in residential use. Markets are held on Mondays (with auction), Tuesdays and Fridays.

The **Bure Valley Railway** is a major attraction, its 15-inch gauge line running for 9 miles (15km) between Aylsham and Wroxham, mainly steam-operated by attractive little locomotives. There are intermediate stations at Brampton, Buxton and Coltishall. The main depot is at Aylsham, where museum, model railway, tourist information, shop, restaurant and picnic area are available to visitors. Services run from April to October, with special events throughout the season. A short distance to the north-west of Aylsham, along the B1354, **Blickling Hall** is a flagship property of the National Trust in East Anglia. The house, of 1616 to 1624, is beautifully symmetrical, with

red brick Jacobean facade and numerous interesting architectural features, particularly the chimneys, all set beside an approach way of great yew hedges. Inside the house there is a wonderful plaster ceiling in the long gallery, a collection of furniture of the eighteenth and nineteenth centuries and an extensive library. There is a legend that Anne Boleyn was born and grew up in an earlier house on the site and that her ghost returns to Blickling each year on the anniversary of her execution. The extensive grounds of nearly 5,000 acres (2,000 hectares) include formal gardens, parkland and lake, all available to visitors for walks, short and not so short. Facilities are comprehensive – shop, restaurant and tea room, plus plant sales.

Heading north along the A140 towards Cromer leads to **Alby Crafts**, by the side of the main road, close to **Erpingham** village. Alby is a working craft centre, promoting mainly British, including much East Anglian, craftsmanship. Set inside restored farm buildings are a bottle museum, paintings, sculpture and ceramics, whilst a 'plantsman's garden' offers 4 acres (2 hectares) of ponds, unusual shrubs, plants and bulbs. A tea room provides drinks and light meals throughout the day. A more unusual attraction is the **Norfolk Children's Book Centre**, a little way further north, by the side of a lane a short distance to the west of the main road.

Situated close together, **Mannington** and **Wolterton** are both stately homes at the smaller end of the scale, family properties of the estate owned by Lord and Lady Walpole, descended from the

The Weavers' Way

This long-distance footpath runs for 57 miles (92km) from Cromer to Great Yarmouth. The name derives from the weaving industry, formerly important in much of Norfolk, which was introduced by Flemish immigrants in the twelfth century. Particular centres were Aylsham, North Walsham, Stalham and Worstead.

Scenically the route is well varied, with the rich farmland and the woodland of North Norfolk contrasting with the grazing marshes of the Norfolk Broads. The National Trust estates of Felbrigg and Blickling are en route and, from Aylsham to Stalham, the trackbed of the former Great Yarmouth to King's Lynn railway line is incorporated. The Broads section of the route passes through Hickling Broad National Nature Reserve and Breydon Water Local Nature Reserve on its way to Great Yarmouth. Here it joins the Angles Way, which runs almost to Thetford. By following the Angles Way, then using the Peddars Way to connect with the Norfolk Coast Path at Holme next the Sea, an enormous circuit can be achieved.

The 'Weavers' Way Challenge' is to walk the length of the Way, accumulating two stamps for each of three zones. A complete card of six stamps qualifies for a special woven badge. The Way was developed by and is managed by Norfolk County Council.

brother of Britain's first prime minister. Public access to both houses is restricted (see 'Places to visit'). There is entry to a small visitor centre, gardens, park, shop and tea room at Mannington and to the parkland at Wolterton. A 'Conservation Trail and Walks Map' is available at Mannington.

Further to the north-west is **Baconsthorpe Castle**, the ruin of a fifteenth-century part-moated, semi-fortified house. Remaining are inner and outer gatehouses and the curtain wall. At Kelling, the **East Anglian Falconry Centre** claims to be the largest in the country, a National Sanctuary, with more than 200 birds of prey, including some rarer species. There are daily flying display, weather permitting. Facilities include play area, café and gift shop.

Holt is without doubt one of the nicest towns in Norfolk, no longer a market town but bustling, with streets, alleys and courtyards well packed with individual shops, inns and cafés. A great fire in 1708 destroyed much of the town, hence the predominance of Georgian buildings. Just outside the town, **Holt Country Park** is a survival of an old heathland area, with a small visitor centre, car parking and walks along waymarked trails.

Paston Way

A 20-mile (30km) route linking Cromer and North Walsham, visiting fifteen villages and fifteen churches (including a few diversions). Based on the Paston family, for centuries landowners in this area and the authors of the 'Paston Letters', correspondence between members of the family from 1422 to 1509, now regarded as a most valuable source of information on the condition of society in those times. Leaflet available from TICs.

Holt station on the edge of town is the terminus of the North Norfolk preserved railway line, with mainly steam-hauled trains to Sheringham (for more details see the entry on Sheringham earlier in this chapter). About 1¼ miles (2km) along the main A148 to the west from Holt is **Letheringsett Watermill**, still producing whole-wheat flour from locally grown wheat. The present mill was built in 1802 on a very ancient mill site and was restored to use in 1982. Working demonstrations are given on most days. Flour is available for purchase at the mill and there is also a gift shop. A little further north along the valley of the River Glaven, the **Natural Surroundings Wild Flower Centre** has 10 acres (4 hectares) devoted to wild flowers and the traditional British countryside, with gardens and nature trail. A small visitor centre also has a shop, plant sales and tea room.

The coast can be rejoined at the pleasant village of Stiffkey or, by bearing more to the right, to **Blakeney**, a little town and former port with an atmosphere all of its own, undoubtedly one of Norfolk's showpieces. Recession of the sea over the centuries has left a network of creeks threading their way through the huge marshes, both salt and freshwater, which separate the town from the distant Blakeney Point, where a nature reserve owned by the National Trust is a prime site for viewing seals, birds and wild flowers. The Blakeney boatmen compete to provide one-hour trips to the Point when the tide is sufficiently high.

Inland are narrow streets, with flower-girt courts and alleyways separating the cottages, a mixture of flint and colour-washed rendered walls. The church of St Nicholas stands massively on its inland hilltop site, with fifteenth-century towers. Inside, there is a lovely old hammer beam roof, graced with angels, and a soaring arch. The old Guildhall, facing the Quay, is built of Flemish bricks. The undercroft has brick vaulting more than 600 years old.

Finally in this chapter is the adjacent village of **Cley-next-the-Sea**, like Wells not now really qualifying for its name but still a place of considerable charm, with its early-eighteenth-century tower mill, which ground corn until 1918, facing the distant sea. At Cley Marshes the coastal nature reserve is the oldest in the country operated by the Norfolk Wildlife Trust. The visitor centre has a small display and shop. There is a beach café close by.

Walks

There is no lack of walking opportunity in this diverse area. The Norfolk Coast Path connects with the Peddars Way (see feature box, Chapter 1) at Holme next the Sea and the Weavers' Way near Cromer (see feature box below). Several lengths of the Coast Path can readily be incorporated into shorter circular walks (see below for example). Many parishes have organised walks within their particular locality.

Above left: Wells-next-the-sea
Above right: Alby Crafts, Erpingham
Below: Felbrigg Courtyard

Other Specimen Walks

1. Mannington Estate

Start from the front of the visitor centre by going along a welcoming grass track towards trees. There are waymarks on a post as the track bends to the left. In less than 100m turn right to cross a wet meadow on boardwalks; there are several routes across the meadow, the objective being to reach rough grass and a little hide at the top end. From the hide, waterfowl on an attractive adjacent pond may be observed.

After the hide, turn right at a white waymark at the end of the meadow, along a wide grass track with several gates/stiles, bearing left across the front of Hall Farm Barn, built in the 1790s and restored about 20 years ago. Opposite the front of the barn turn sharp right, to walk along a field boundary, with Mannington Hall in view ahead. A stile in 40m gives a choice for the next part of the route; go over this and turn right or continue along the edge of the meadow.

On reaching a minor road turn right and then, in 50m, turn left at an iron gate with waymark. A lovely path now winds through largely coppiced woodland, another important wildlife habitat. Turn right at a clearing, go over a little footbridge and stile and follow the edge of Bridge Meadow, in the process of being returned to its original state. As the track bends to the left, ignore a stile on the right.

Opposite a post with many waymarks, turn right into a tunnel through the foliage and along an attractive green lane, rising gently between banks rich in bramble. Go straight on at a junction to reach the edge of Mossymere Wood. (A diversion through the wood along a waymarked path adds to the walk; it is essential to keep bearing right to return to the main route close to a dwelling.)

Continue as the track bends to the right to head north. Pass a dwelling on the left, then a part-ruinous farm building, and continue to join the public road. Turn right to return to the visitor centre in approximately 400yds/m.

2. Blakeney and Cley

There are a few parking places by the quay in Blakeney. From the eastern end of the quay walk inland, up High Street. There are two car parks which might be preferred to the quayside parking, particularly at busy periods. Go straight across the A149 into Wiveton Road, passing the church with its massive tower. Follow the road, between cornfields with bindweed and field-edge poppies adding colour. The Bell Inn is soon reached, facing Wiveton Church across a green. Most of Wiveton village is to the left.

Go straight on, following a 'Cley' signpost downhill to a bridge over the River Glaven. Turn left at a crossroads with a 'Cley 1' signpost and go along a minor road, passing reclaimed marshland to the left, to reach a large green with an inn and St Margaret's church, Cley, with its fine high nave and clerestory and many interesting features, behind.

Turn right, to rise through the churchyard, then exit by a small gate, turning left along a surfaced lane leading into the main part of Cley, passing the Village Hall on the right. The road becomes a cul de sac, with a pottery down a track on the left. Just as further progress seems to be barred, and the road loses its surface, go round to the left. In 20m follow a little sign on the right 'to Cley Mill and High Street', going under an arch to the main road. Go straight across and take the unmade roadway to visit the windmill.

From the windmill return to the main road and turn right to pass several shops. Go round a sharp right-hand bend at a road junction and then, in 50m, go up a few steps on the right at a signpost reading 'Blakeney, 4km/2½ miles, Norfolk Coast Path'. The route is now very simple to follow along coastal defence embankments. Cross the river on a footbridge and shortly turn right at a gate/stile towards the sea. The view of Cley Mill from the embankment is very fine.

Turn left at a junction with a 'Protection of Sea Defences' notice. On reaching a wide creek, with shingle beach beyond, turn left to continue along the top of the embankment. Far to the right is the hull of a beached ship, as the path bears to the left to head for Blakeney. Bear left at a junction, pass another wreck and then a small waterfowl reserve to reach Blakeney Quay close to the public conveniences.

Cycle Rides

As with Norfolk generally, this is fine cycling country. The Marriott's Way, based on Reepham, has already been described above and the Norfolk Coast Cycleway follows quiet roads and lanes through varied countryside between King's Lynn and Cromer. Copies of a detailed map/guide to this designated and marked route are available from Tourist Information Centres in the coastal area. The Wensum Valley cycling routes are very close to the western fringe.

Cycle hire is widespread throughout the area. Check with tourist information centres for up-to-date information.

Car Tours

From north-east Norfolk, practically the whole of East Anglia is within reach for those who enjoy long excursions. Readily to hand are the towns and villages of the north coast, Norwich, Great Yarmouth and the Norfolk Broads.

Public Transport

The only remaining railway service is on the 'Bittern Line', connecting Sheringham, Cromer and Norwich, with seven intermediate stops, including North Walsham, Worstead and Wroxham. Trains are at approximately hourly intervals (two-hourly on Sundays).

Bus services are more plentiful; the information in the previous chapter concerning the long-distance coastal service applies equally to the area covered by this chapter. For information call Traveline (Tel. 0870 48 49 50).

The showing of a valid bus or rail ticket entitles the bearer to a discounted admission charge at many of the visitor attractions.

Above: Blickling Hall
Right: Dinosaur Park
Below: Holt Station

Places to Visit

In and around Sheringham and Cromer

North Norfolk Railway *W*

☎ 01263 820 800
Preserved railway line from Sheringham to Holt. Services every month other than January. Mainly steam-hauled trains.

Sheringham Little Theatre *W*

☎ 01263 822347 (box office)
Performances from early May to late Sep.

Sheringham Museum *W*

☎ 01263 821871
Open from mid-April to late Oct, Mon to Sat and Bank Holiday weekends, 10am–4pm.

Fishermen's Heritage Centre *W*

7–8 Westcliff, Sheringham.
☎ 01263 824343
Open daily, Easter to Sep, noon to 5pm.

Norfolk Shire Horse Centre *W*

West Runton.
☎ 01263 837339
Facilities for the disabled. Open from late Mar to the end of Oct, daily except Sat, 10am–5pm.

Priory Maze and Gardens

Beeston Regis
☎ 01263 822986
Ten acres of attractive gardens, including the only hedge maze in Norfolk. Tea room and plant centre. Open Apr to Oct, 10am–5pm.

The Muckleburgh Collection *W*

Weybourne
☎ 01263 588210
The UK's largest privately owned museum of military vehicles. Working demonstrations. Facilities for the disabled. Open daily from April to October and at February school half-term (Sundays only from late Feb to late Mar), 10am–5pm.

Cromer Museum *W*

Tucker Street
☎ 01263 513543
Open daily, Apr to Oct, weekdays 10am–5pm, Sun 2–5pm. Telephone for dates/times out of season.

Pavilion Theatre *W*

Cromer
☎ 01263 512495
Seaside variety shows
Open from mid-June to mid-Sep.

Felbrigg Hall, Gardens and Park *W*

(National Trust)
☎ 01263 837444
Shop and refreshments. Facilities for the disabled
Open (hall and gardens) from end of March to the beginning of Nov, daily except Thu and Fri, hall 1–5pm, gardens 11am–5pm, estate dawn to dusk every day except Christmas Day.

Places to Visit

In and around Mundesley, North Walsham and Reepham

Mundesley Maritime Museum

Operated by volunteers
Open from May to Sep, Thu and Sat 10am–4pm, other days including Sundays 10am–3pm.

Stow Windmill   W

(on B1159 just outside Mundesley)
☎ 01263 720298
Built 1825/7, this corn mill operated until 1930. Art gallery and shop
Open daily from 10am to dusk.

Dinosaur Adventure Park

Lenwade
☎ 01603 870245
Adventure play areas, crazy golf, refreshments, picnic area.
Open from early April to early September, daily from 10am. From early Sep to beginning of Oct, Fri, Sat and Sun only.

Norfolk Motorcycle Museum   W

North Walsham
☎ 01692 406266
Open daily 10am–4.30pm. Closed on Sundays from Oct to Easter.

The Animal Ark

Great Witchingham
☎ 01603 872274
Adventure play area, tea room, gift shop and picnic areas
Open daily, 10am–5pm.

Reepham Station

☎ 01603 871187
Marriott's Way and refreshments. Shop and shop museum
Open from 10am–5pm except at Christmas and New Year.

From Aylsham to Cley

Bure Valley Railway   W

Aylsham
☎ 01263 733858
Narrow-gauge, mainly steam-hauled railway line. Museum, model railway, restaurant, picnic area, shop, tourist information
Services operate from April to September (and during school half-term holidays in Feb and Oct, with 'Santa Specials' pre-Christmas).

Blickling Hall   W

(National Trust)
☎ 01263 738030
Stately Home. Shop, restaurant and tea room
Open (house) from early April to July, Wed to Sun and Bank Holiday Mondays, 1–5pm; August, Wed to Mon 1–5pm; garden same days as house, 10.15am–5.15pm plus Nov to Mar, Thu to Sun 11am–4pm; park and woods daily all year, dawn to dusk.

Alby Crafts   W

near Erpingham
☎ 01263 761590
Craft centre. Gift shop and tea room
Open from mid-Jan to late Dec, Tue to Sun and Bank Holidays, 10am–5pm.

Norfolk Children's Book Centre   *W*

Alby, near Erpingham
☎ 01263 761402
Open Mon to Sat, 10am–4pm, closed bank holidays.

Wolterton Park   *W*

☎ 01263 584175
Stately home and visitor centre with information display and toilets
House open Fridays, Apr to Oct, 2–4pm (last entry). Park open every day from 9am to dusk.

Mannington Gardens   *W*

near Little Barningham
☎ 01263 584175
Gardens of stately home and surrounding estate land. Tea rooms
Gardens open May to Sep, Sundays 11am–5pm; also Wed to Fri, Jun to Aug.

Baconsthorpe Castle

near Holt
Castle ruins
Open daily from 10am–4pm.

East Anglian Falconry Centre

Kelling
Play area, café and gift shop. Open daily in summer 10am–5pm; Oct to Mar weekends only, 10am–3pm.

North Norfolk Railway   *W*

Holt
Mainly steam-hauled preserved railway line. Refer to Sheringham section for details.

Letheringsett Watermill   *W*

near Holt
☎ 01263 713153
Milling demonstrations and shop
Open all year, Whitsun to early September, Mon to Fri 10am–5pm, Sat 9am–1pm; Sep to Whitsun, Mon to Fri 9am–4pm, Sat 9am–1pm.

Natural Surroundings Wild Flower Centre

near Holt
☎ 01263 711091
Plant sales, gardens, woodland trails, animals
Open all year, generally Tue to Sun 10am–5pm. Reduced opening days/hours out of season.

Langham Glass   *W*

East Rudham, Fakenham
☎ 01485 529111
Demonstrations, museum and video, shop and refreshments
Open all year, 7 days a week, 10am–5pm (closed weekends out of season).

Blakeney Point

Boat trips from Blakeney or Morston, particularly for seal viewing
☎ 01263 740038 or 01263 740701 or 01263 740791.

Blakeney Guildhall

(English Heritage)
☎ 0845 3006116
Open at any reasonable time
☎ 01263 740008.

Cley Marshes Nature Reserve

Visitor centre. Gift shop and refreshments. Disabled access
Open all year round (closed Mon other then Bank Holidays). Visitor centre open late Mar to early Dec, 10am–5pm.

The highly distinctive area of the Norfolk Broads is probably better known to the world at large than any other part of East Anglia. Perhaps even more than the Fens it has come to typify a general impression of the whole area; flat and with a great deal of water. In comparatively recent years this unique landscape has been added to the distinguished company of the National Parks, hopefully giving the consequent extra protection and resources to safeguard its future.

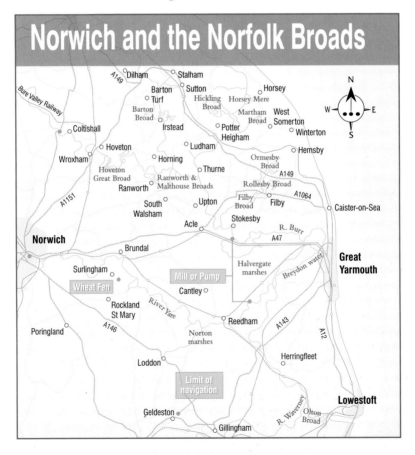

Norwich and the Norfolk Broads

Although the area is always referred to as the 'Norfolk Broads', the southern part is actually in Suffolk. For the purpose of this guide it makes no sense to attempt an apportionment and a small part of the latter county is, therefore, included in this chapter. In terms of planning an itinerary it is more appropriate to consider the north – the rivers Bure, Ant and Thurne and their associated broads – and then the south – the Rivers Yare, Waveney and Chet and their associated broads.

The Broads has immense visitor potential, obviously dominated by boating holidays, but not forgetting the importance of Great Yarmouth and, above all, the wonderful city of Norwich. The shape of the following itinerary is, inevitably, strongly influenced by the layout of the rivers and the many lakes, both large and small, collectively known as the 'Broads', which in this area have a profound effect on road communications, resulting in some very roundabout routes.

Norwich

A good place to start is **Norwich**, the 'capital' of East Anglia, said by Nicholas Pevsner, with only a little exaggeration, 'to have everything' strategically situated at the hub of a network of major roads and of railway services, at the western end of the Broads holiday area. By city standards Norwich is compact, with the great majority of the attractive and interesting features within easy walking distance of one another and of car parks, bus and railway stations. For attractions outside the city centre, local bus services are good.

The origins of Norwich go back to well before the Norman Conquest; coins minted early in the tenth century carry the name of the city and, by the time of the conquest, the city was one of England's largest, with a population of well over five thousand. In early times the development of the wool trade increased local prosperity, as did the fertile surrounding countryside. The rivers Wensum and Yare combined to give a navigable route to the sea at the present Great Yarmouth.

Despite the general material prosperity, the city and its area have, over the centuries, seen more than their fair share of strife. In 1272, disagreement over the levying of tolls on animal fairs by the then dominant monastery resulted in riots and a citizens versus monks pitched battle. The Mayor was killed during the Peasants' Revolt in 1381 and 'Kett's Rebellion' against the enclosure of common land in 1549 was very much a Norfolk affair. After the latter rebellion was put down, Robert Kett was hanged from the walls of the castle. In the calmer times of the late sixteenth century, many skilled weavers arrived from the Netherlands and were involved in the revival of the textile industry.

Today's reminders of the city's history are very fine indeed. The Norman **cathedral** is one of England's greatest, started at the end of the eleventh century by the first Bishop of Norwich, Herbert de Losinga. The distinctive white stone of the exterior was imported from Caen, in Normandy, ending its water-borne journey along a little canal connecting the cathedral to the nearby river, dug especially for this purpose. Inside the cathedral, among many fine features, the roof of the nave is of particular interest, with detailed viewing aided by mirrors. A stone effigy, probably of about AD 1100, fourteenth-century wall paintings by local artists and the cloisters all rank highly in visitor interest. The 315ft (96m) spire, second only to Salisbury in Britain's cathedrals, was added at the end of the fifteenth century.

Close to the south door is the simple grave of Nurse Edith Cavell, shot by the Germans in 1916 for helping the escape of Allied prisoners from occupied Belgium. Running down to the river at Pull's Ferry, the Cathedral Close and Ferry Lane have a wealth of good buildings. The Ferry is long gone; the wharf here served the monastic community at the cathedral and was the start point of the ancient canal.

Almost as old as the cathedral, the construction of the great Norman **castle** was started early in the twelfth century, with the walls again being of Caen stone, re-faced with Bath stone in 1834–9. The huge keep now looks rather less than warlike in its use as a museum and gallery Additional defences for the city were provided in the fourteenth century, when 20ft (6m) walls were erected, with ten fortified gateways and a series of towers, now best seen at Carrow Hill, where a section of wall climbs to Black Tower.

Other survivals of early times include **Strangers Hall** (early fourteenth century) and the finely carved **Erpingham Gate** of 1420, opposite the cathedral west front, donated by Sir Thomas Erpingham who commanded the archers at the battle of Agincourt and features in Shakespeare's *Henry V*.

Beside the cathedral is King Edward VI School and a statue of the most famous pupil, Horatio (later Lord) Nelson, whose education certainly seems to have been spread around Norfolk.

Modern Norwich is closely integrated into the ancient framework. Indeed the recent **Castle Mall** shopping centre, with entrances close to the Market Square, is brilliantly incorporated into the mound beside the castle, with its elegant glass and iron roof forming part of the 4 acres (1.6 hectares) of public space, mainly grass, water features and promenades, enhanced by the partially outdoor cafés of the shopping centre. Norwich was a pioneer of city centre pedestrianisation, which now contributes a great deal to the enjoyment of wandering along the narrow old streets, where speciality shops and restaurants complement the city's major department stores.

The huge marketplace is central, sitting below the City Hall, opened by King George VI in 1938. To one side is the early-fifteenth-century **Guildhall**. To the other side is **St. Peter Mancroft**, with perpendicular architecture, one of the finest of the city's many churches. Close to St Peter Mancroft is the **Forum**, an ultra-modern building with Tourist Information, public library, 'Origins' exhibition and café. Towards the edge of the city centre, quite close to the cathedral, the short, hilly, little street known as **Elm Hill** has a wonderful old world atmosphere, with cobble-paving and timber-framed colour-washed buildings, housing galleries, antique shops and a pottery.

Having absorbed the overall charm, there are many specific attractions worthy of mention. The **Castle Museum** is a major feature. The extensive collection includes the art, archaeology and natural history of Norfolk. Paintings focus strongly on the Norfolk School, headed by John Crome and John Sell Cotman, supplemented by a good collection of seventeenth-century Dutch and Flemish work. The museum also has the world's finest collection of Lowestoft porcelain, as well as weapons and musical instruments. There are periodic visiting exhibitions of importance. On the same site are the Regimental Museum of the Royal Norfolk Regiment and the Whistler Theatre.

A notable feature of Norwich is the extensive use made of redundant churches. **St Peter, Hungate**, which has a fifteenth-century hammer beam roof, houses religious arts and crafts. St Michael's church in Coslany Street has **Inspire**, a 'hands-on' science centre with many interesting exhibits and constructions for the young and the not so young.

Quite different is the **Mustard Shop** in the arcade connecting the Market Square with the Castle Mall complex. The history of Colman's mustard is displayed. In Bridewell Street the **Bridewell Museum** occupies a building which was a prison for beggars and tramps. **Dragon Hall** in King Street was hidden from view for five centuries. This splendid medieval cloth merchant's hall, with timber framing and a superb crown post roof, has been restored and is open to the public. Cinema City, the Playhouse and the Maddergate Theatre provide a range of entertainment.

Outside the city centre are two further attractions of note. At the University of East Anglia, the **Sainsbury Centre for Visual Arts** is a modern gallery in a modern building, the first major design by Norman Foster, which visitors may either love or hate. Here, the collection of Robert and Lisa Sainsbury includes a great deal of modern western art and fine arts from all over the world. Featuring strongly are Francis Bacon, Henry Moore and Alberto Giacometti. Secondly, and on a more modest scale, is the **City of Norwich Aviation Museum** at Old

Norwich Forum

Above: Norwich Market
Right: Colemans Mustard Shop, Norwich

Norwich Road, Horsham St Faith. Aircraft, engines, memorabilia and a display of the local role of the US Air Force are on display in a constantly improving collection.

Public parks and open spaces feature strongly in Norwich, with a Jun/Jul season of free open-air theatre at five venues. The river also plays its part, with a popular riverside footpath. **River cruises** include the Wensum and part of the Broads and there is a river bus from Elm Hill to Thorpe Station.

An efficient 'Park and Ride' system with six centres outside the city (Harford, Costessey, Thickthorn, Airport, Sprowston and Postwick) is a great asset for visitors preferring to leave their vehicles outside the busy centre. Daytime guided walking tours of about 1½ hours' duration are available from Apr to Oct. Themed evening tours operate from May to Aug (details from the TIC, ☎ 01603 727927).

Nelson statue in Norwich

From Brundall to Stalham

Due east of Norwich, on the north bank of the River Yare, **Brundall** has little to attract the visitor. Close by, however, the **Strumpshaw Steam Museum**, close to the river bank, has a large collection of steam engines, lorries, working mechanical organs and narrow-gauge railway.

A few miles to the north-east of Norwich, the small town of **Wroxham** is a popular holiday centre by the side of the River Bure, its popularity very much anchored on pleasure boating, with abundant boatyards and moorings. Roy's of Wroxham is world famous as the 'biggest village store in Britain', in fact an emporium occupying several buildings in Wroxham, with some branches elsewhere. Always busy in season, Wroxham also has the southern terminus of the Bure Valley Railway, a narrow-gauge, largely steam-hauled line (see under Aylsham in Chapter 2), a variety of river/broad tours on large launches, and small craft of many types for day and part-day hire. The adjacent village of Hoveton shares a common boundary at the bridge over the River Bure; many of the facilities are, in fact, in Hoveton, but this need not concern the visitor, as the name 'Wroxham' can serve for both. There is a railway station on the 'Bittern Line' which connects Sheringham, Cromer and Norwich.

A short diversion to the west leads to **Coltishall**, a large village on the River Bure, notable as the head of navigation for pleasure cruisers on that river. There is a strong World War II RAF and US Air Force history in this area, as in so much of East Anglia. Coltishall has a station on the Bure Valley Railway.

Three miles (5km) north of Wroxham, **Wroxham Barns** is a major rural craft centre, with many kinds of workshop, gift shops and tea rooms, augmented by Williamson's Traditional Family Fair and a junior farm. Close by, **Hoveton Hall Gardens** and tea rooms offer a very fine garden, rich in rhododendrons and hydrangeas, with an attractive lake.

Horning is a substantial village along the side of the River Bure below Wroxham. The street hugging close to the river is quite pretty and is well defined by an inn at each end. The Ferry Inn is a Broads focal point, with plentiful moorings adjacent, obviously popular with the boating fraternity. Continuing away from Wroxham, next is Ludham Bridge, with moorings, shop and cafe. **Ludham** village is well provided with shops, inn and tea room. Close by, Womack Water, with boatyard and moorings, connects with the River Thurne. St Catherine's Church is fifteenth-century, with a fourteenth-century chancel. Inside are a hammer beam roof, quaint carving on the chancel arch, a screen of 1493 with paintings of saints and a striking well-carved fifteenth-century font. Occupying a lonely site by the side of the River Thurne, the ruins of **St Benet's Abbey**, with the odd superimposition of the tower of a windmill, can be reached from Ludham. A better approach to the abbey is by river.

Minor roads to the north-west from Ludham lead to **How Hill**. Here, the house is used as a residential Broads Study Centre. Apart from the gardens,

the adjacent land is open to the public with plenty of space for picnics. **Toad Hole Cottage**, down by the River Ant, has been refurbished as a nineteenth-century eel-catcher's cottage. From the adjacent landing stage the *Electric Eel*, an eight-seater boat, operates fifty-minute trips, gliding almost silently along the dykes among the traditional reed beds, with excellent viewing of the abundant wildlife.

From Horning a minor road heads up the west side of **Barton Broad,** weaving in and out to visit tiny villages and hamlets, such as Irstead, Nettishead (with inn) and Barton Turf, after which the main A1151 road must be joined, turning right to Wayford Bridge and on to Stalham. There are two nature reserves on this side of the Broad.

Situated at the northern extremity of the Broads, **Stalham** is one of the smaller, quieter Norfolk towns, with a small market each Tue. The one long street has inns and restaurants and a fair range of individual shops, bounded by the church at one end and the post office at the other. Boats reach the town by a channel at the north end of Barton Broad; there are staithes and a small boat building industry. **The Museum of the Broads** has an extensive display of boats and other aspects of traditional life on the Broads.

From Sutton to Ranworth

Sutton and its well-known windmill are a short distance to the south from Stalham. The mill is claimed to be the tallest in Britain, with nine floors and a viewing gallery. Much milling machin-

Above: St Benet's Abbey
Left: Caister Castle

ery is still in situ but the mill is likely to be closed whilst subject to a long-term renovation programme. Over 200 years old, it remained in use until 1940. Close by, in Church Road, is the small but interesting **Sutton Pottery**, where work in progress can be watched.

From Sutton, minor roads lead across country to **Hickling**. At the north end of Hickling Broad, the Pleasure Boat Inn at Hickling Heath has moorings and Broad exploration trips in a small boat. Two miles (3km) further on, with some care in the route finding, is the **Hickling Broad Nature Reserve Visitor Centre**, operated by the Norfolk Wildlife Trust. Colour way-marked trails, some with boardwalks, wind through reed beds and marshes beside the Broad, among a wealth of wildlife. The Visitor Centre has the usual information, gift shop, hot and cold drinks and ice cream.

Most of this part of the Norfolk coast is without significant features, a long line of sea defences backing a sandy beach. Sea Palling lies just inland, with an inn; at the nearby seafront another inn is accompanied by a few shops of post-war construction, with watersports on the award-winning beach. The coast road (B1159) continues to Horsey and **Horsey Mill**, the latter owned by the National Trust, with car park, public conveniences and the small Staithe Stores where hot and cold drinks and ice cream may be purchased. The former drainage mill of 1912 was struck by lightning in 1943 and put out of action. The tower is noted for its views and there is surviving machinery.

To return to the coast from Sutton, head for **Winterton-on-Sea**, where the church tower is visible from well out to sea, and the beach is backed by an inn, car park and public conveniences. Continuing to the south, Hemsby, Newport, Scratby and California all have extensive holiday park-type visitor accommodation, with appropriate, shops, catering and amusements.

Caister-on-Sea is a much larger, largely modern, residential town with a small shopping centre, separated from Great Yarmouth by the racecourse and not much else. Perhaps surprisingly the town has Roman origins. Helped by the brown road signs, the site of the Roman camp is not difficult to find; the key is the roundabout where the B1159 joins the A149 on the inland edge of the town.

Just inland of Caister, the A1064 leads to the well-signposted privately owned **Caister Castle Car Collection**, with more than 200 exhibits housed in a purpose-built large exhibition centre in the grounds attached to the ruins of the medieval Caister Castle. The main A149 to Rollesby, bypassing Ormesby St Margaret, soon reaches the **Norfolk Rare Breeds Centre** at Decoy Farm House, Ormesby St Michael, where rare breeds of cattle, sheep, pigs and other farm and domestic animals are on display.

Martham is a large village, pleasant enough, with some Georgian houses in the middle, but not of particular visitor interest. For those who like to seek out quiet backwaters, there is a lane to the north leading in two thirds of a mile (1km) to the River Thurne at Martham Ferry (no operational ferry), with moorings along Martham Staithe.

Potter Heigham is a key centre in

the northern part of the Broads, with extensive boatyards and all boating facilities. The road bridge over the River Thurne has long been notorious as a test of steely nerves for amateur helmsmen steering a large cruiser through with literally inches to spare, whilst top-deck sunbathers leap for safety. Potter Heigham divides naturally into three communities: the boating area by the bridge, with visitor-type shops and cafés; the small old village two thirds of a mile (1km) to the north-west; and a detached residential area on the northeast side of the A149. Heading back in a southerly direction, a turn to the west reaches **Thurne** hamlet in an isolated position by the side of the river, with inn, moorings and a well-known windmill. Minor roads lead through Burgh St Margaret to Filby, where a lane to the south reaches **Thrigby Hall Wildlife Gardens** in approximately one mile (1.5km). A well-presented collection of Asian animals and birds occupies the grounds of the Hall, an attractive old building. Tigers, monkeys, crocodiles, alligators and storks are all well represented. There is a children's play area and the usual visitor facilities.

Returning to the main A1064, the River Bure is crossed at Acle Bridge (moorings and inn) to reach the area to the south of that river and of the series of Broads which block road communication between this area and Horning/Ludham. **Acle** is a small town with a fair range of shops and a market on Thus. There are moorings at Acle Dyke, connecting to the River Bure. The Stracey Arms windpump, with the inn adjacent, is nearly 3 miles (5km) downstream. **Stokesby**, on the north bank of the river, is a pleasant riverside village, with green and moorings.

North-west of Acle, close to the modest village of South Walsham, **Fairhaven Woodland and Water Gardens**, of 170 acres (70 hectares), were developed in 1947 by Lord Fairhaven into an attractive area, retaining the original dykes by the edge of South Walsham Broad. The gardens are seen at their best in spring and early summer.

Ranworth Broad is barred to pleasure boats and is now of national and international importance for wildlife, forming part of the large Bure Marshes National Nature Reserve. A nature trail leads through woodland and reed beds (boardwalk) to the floating **conservation centre**, well equipped and with extensive views over the open water (binoculars provided). Common tern, great crested grebe and, in winter, teal, widgeon, shoveller, pochard and gadwall come here to feed. The Broad is also an inland roost for cormorants.

Great Yarmouth

The most southerly and shortest itinerary of this chapter starts at **Great Yarmouth**, which can be regarded as three places in one. Firstly, a port facing inland across the River Yare, backed by the unlovely industrial/commercial area of the Denes; secondly, a sizeable market town with a good shopping centre and large residential suburbs; and thirdly, a major holiday and visitor resort with a long Marine Parade behind a sandy beach, two piers and the usual range of seaside attractions.

The site of the town is a spit of land between the Yare and the North Sea, formed many centuries ago by progressive silting. The Romans had a presence at neighbouring Caister-on-Sea, but in Great Yarmouth itself it is medieval remains which are apparent. Sections of the old town wall are best seen at the **North West Tower** of 1344, close to the river, a little way north of the most northerly of the road bridges across the river, and a short distance behind St Nicholas' Church. The Tower is now a small museum. South of the Market Place and behind South Quay was an area of congested courts and alleys called The Rows, 145 in total, set out in a grid pattern which still defines the shape of this part of the town, although damage during World War II was considerable. On South Quay itself, a row of Tudor, Georgian and Victorian buildings combines to form a handsome inland-facing waterfront.

Featuring in this area is **The Elizabethan House** at 4 South Quay, a sixteenth-century merchant's house, now a museum of domestic life. Close by are the **Row 111 House** and the **Old Merchant's House,** owned by English Heritage and operated as a joint attraction, contrasting the housing of the richer and the poorer classes in this area. There are good plaster ceilings and an exhibition of historic local architectural fittings. Entrance is by guided tour only. The thirteenth-century **Greyfriars Cloisters**, with some early wall paintings, is part of the same visitor complex. Comparatively recent in the same part of South Quay is the **Norfolk Nelson Museum**. Close behind South Quay are two further museums – the **Time and Tide Museum** of Great Yarmouth Life in Blackfriars Road and the **Historic Smokehouse Museum** and Great Yarmouth Potteries in Trinity Place.

In nearby Tolhouse Street, the late-thirteenth-century **Tolhouse** is said to be the oldest civic building in Britain. The dungeons are open to the public, as is a local history museum and brass rubbing centre. The *Lydia Eve*, last of the once numerous steam drifter fishing boats, is periodically moored at South Quay as a visitor attraction. This wealth of visitor attractions on and around South Quay is well laid out in a leaflet obtainable from the Tourist Information Centre on Marine Parade (☎ 01493 846345).

More modern Great Yarmouth is centred on the vast Market Place (markets on Wed, Sat and summer Fris), with a shopping area which includes the odd elegant arcade. The large twelfth-century parish church of St Nicholas, restored after a World War II fire, is at the north end. Adjacent, in a timber-framed cottage. is the birthplace of Anna Sewell, of *Black Beauty* fame. At the north-east corner of the Market Place is the group of almshouses called the **Fishermen's Hospice**, restored and improved in 1985/6, for 'decayed fishermen'. The draconian rules governing the behaviour of the residents are set out on a noticeboard.

On the seafront are the **Great Yarmouth Maritime Museum**, displaying the story of the local coast, and **Amazonia**, the world of reptiles. Perhaps unexpectedly, in Great Yarmouth there is yet another Nelson link. He stands isolated on a column soaring above the mediocre surroundings of the Denes area on which he is condemned to gaze in perpetuity.

The holiday resort really needs little further description as it does its best to emulate Blackpool. Theatres, sports and leisure centre, racecourses for horses and greyhounds, pleasure beach, sea life centre, stock car racing and amusement arcades all compete to entertain the visitor. The town has railway services to Norwich and beyond, with a choice of route through the Broads countryside.

Inland from Great Yarmouth

The area immediately inland from Great Yarmouth is rich in visitor interest. **Burgh Castle** is the site of the Roman fort Gariannonum, situated on a mound which towers over the flat marshes by the head of Breydon Water, with the Berney Arms Mill, a noted Broadland landmark, clearly in view. From the car park at the entrance to Church Farm, the fort is less than half a mile (1km) on foot. A Norman motte and bailey castle was superimposed on the Roman site; strong stone walls, up to about 16 feet (5m) in height, survive on three sides of the rectangle, the fourth side having slid down the steep western slope. There is a burial ground to the east of the fort.

Fritton parish church has a round tower with a Norman base and a fifteenth-century top. The nave roof is thatched. Inside is a restored early-sixteenth-century oak screen with old paintings, carved font and triple-decker pulpit. **Fritton Lake Countryworld** has a large lake with rowing boats, nine-hole golf course, putting, railway, craft centre, pony rides, waterfowl, falconry displays, children's farmyard and adventure playground.

Somerleyton Hall and twelve acres of garden feature a famous maze, established in yew in 1846, good statuary and the Loggia Tea Rooms An early Victorian mansion, the Hall is the home of Lord and Lady Somerleyton. There is a strong Italian influence in the design, with a great deal of carved stone. Some state rooms are very fine, with pictures by Landseer and Wright of Derby. Woodcarving by Grinling Gibbons and glasshouses by Paxton are also featured.

Herringfleet Smock Mill of the1830s was the last operational mill of its type. It stands beside the River Waveney and can be reached by an easy footpath, mainly across grazing marshes, but with several gates and stiles to negotiate. The distance is less than half a mile (1km). The footpath is signposted by the side of the B1074, less than half a mile (1km) north-west of Herringfleet church. There is a small parking lay-by adjacent.

The ruins of **St Olave's Priory** are found a short distance along a rough track to the right, approximately 150m on the Yarmouth side of the road bridge across the River Waveney. There is a good deal of rare medieval brickwork including a notable refectory undercroft with fan brick vaulting dating from about 1300. At the Dissolution only a prior and five canons remained. If the undercroft door is locked, the key is obtainable from Priory House nearby. Once having crossed the River Waveney at St Olave's, visitor attractions are rather more thin on the ground.

The A143 leads towards **Beccles**,

a busy Suffolk market town but very much part of the Broadland scene. Following major fires in the sixteenth and seventeenth centuries, Beccles is now a mellow town of red-brick Georgian houses, many showing Dutch influence. The 97ft (30m) tall bell tower of the parish church of St Michael stands apart from the main building. Also of interest are the eighteenth-century octagonal town hall and the **Town Museum** in Ballygate. The latter occupies a beautiful building with displays of social aspects of life in the town. On Newgate, William Clowes Ltd have operated a printing business since 1870. The comprehensive **printing museum** was established in 1984 to commemorate the 400th anniversary of the granting of the town's charter. The Quay is an important boating centre quite close to the head of navigation on the Waveney, which is at Geldeston lock, about 3 miles (4.5km) further upriver. The Quay has an inn, information centre, public conveniences and children's play area all close to the extensive boat moorings. Beccles railway station has services on the line connecting Ipswich and Lowestoft.

Although a little way above the limit of Broadland boating, it is logical to include **Bungay** as part of the Broads. A compact market town, clustering tightly around its Market Place, with a butter cross dating from 1689, Bungay has a fair array of shops, with antiques well represented. A disastrous fire in 1688 means that most of the older property is of the eighteenth century. **Bigod**

Bungay Market Cross

Castle was built in 1165 and extended in 1294 by members of the family of the same name, powerful Suffolk landowners of the time. By the late fourteenth century it had already become ruinous. A gatehouse, bridge pit and curtain walling remain on site. Other small remnants may be found in the town.

The small **Bungay Museum** is situated in the Council Offices in Broad Street. Two rooms are used to display coins and miscellaneous local relics.

At nearby **Earsham**, the **Otter Trust** has a large collection of British and Asian otters in a series of spacious paddocks with good viewing facilities.

The Norfolk Broads

Two thousand years ago there was a vast and complex estuary with its mouth between present day Caister-on-Sea and the high ground at Burgh Castle, extending inland for several miles up what are now the rivers Bure, Ant, Yare and Waveney. The formation of a shingle spit partially blocked the mouth of this estuary, forcing the waters of the Rivers Yare and Bure to divert to the south. Progressive silting followed and, by the time of the Norman conquest, the fishing community of Yarmouth was established on the spit.

The Broads is often thought of as a fine 'natural' landscape; like the great majority of English landscapes, this is far from the truth. Twentieth-century research has revealed that extensive peat digging in medieval times created huge but shallow hollows into which water subsequently seeped, creating the numerous lakes large and small now collectively known as the Broads. The study of monastic records has helped in this discovery; in the early fourteenth century Norwich Cathedral Priory purchased something like 400,000 turves as fuel. The rising water levels inevitably killed off the digging process.

The succeeding centuries saw the development of a distinct way of life among the lakes, the dykes and the huge beds of sedge and reed. Fishing, eel and duck catching and the cutting of the reed and sedge provided work and a living for the sparse population. The need to produce food from the land to supplement that obtained from nature led to a great deal of drainage of the marshes by systems of dykes and windpumps, many of which remain as a highly characteristic feature of the Broads landscape. In this way, grazing marshes were created. In modern times the traditional industries have faded as the build-up of sewage wastes, agricultural chemicals and pollution of all types from the intensive use by pleasure boats has adversely affected water quality and has reduced the richness and diversity of plant and animal life. Open water is now much less and the gradual conversion of the edges to fen, then carr (largely alder), then oak woodland, is proceeding steadily. Some years ago a start was made in attempting to restore areas of the unique wetland habitat by improving water quality to allow the return of the original vegetation and the associated wildlife. Cockshoot Broad is an example of what can be achieved.

Perhaps the most important factor in protecting this unique environment is the achievement of a status equivalent to a National Park in 1989, bringing stronger planning controls and better targeting of resources.

Village signs

Three lakes with waterfowl, muntjac deer, fallow deer and wallabies add to the interest. A few kilometres to the north, **Raveningham** has extensive gardens surrounding the elegant Georgian house, providing the setting for many rare and unusual plants, with sculptures, parkland and church.

Further to the west, **Loddon** and **Chedgrave** are substantial villages on either side of the River Chet. The quay at Loddon was formerly of commercial importance and the village retains considerable charm. **Reedham** is an important communication point, with a well-known chain ferry across the River Yare and a railway junction. Beside the ferry crossing the inn is a lively place in season. The well-preserved large but lonely mill at Berney Arms can be reached by car, by train to the halt about ten minutes' walk away, or by boat. The mill is the tallest (seven floors) remaining marsh mill in working order.

Station 146 Control Tower at Seething Airfield is south-east of Poringland, off the B1332 Norwich to Bungay road. The restored control tower has relics of the US Air Force 448th bomb group which operated with Liberator aircraft from this airfield during World War II. At **Poringland**, the Play Barn indoor and outdoor activity centre offers a wide range of activities for children, particularly those of seven years and under. In summer the activities include pony and tractor/trailer rides.

Walks

The Broads area is well provided with short walks based on nature trails. A good example is at Hickling Broad, where a one-mile (1.5km) trail from the visitor centre to the edge of the Broad is partly on boardwalk, partly on gravel and partly on grass, traversing an area rich in wildlife.

The Weavers' Way winds through the area of the Broads from Great Yarmouth to North Walsham before heading west to Aylsham and then north to join the Norfolk Coast Path near Cromer.

Horsey Mill

A good example of a modest walk of just under 5 miles (7.5km) is based on Horsey Mill. Start at the National Trust car park by the mill. Cross the road by the car park entrance, then the bridge over the ditch, and go over a stile. Follow the well-marked path along the edge of a field, heading towards the coast. Go over a waymarked stile to turn left beside a drainage ditch.

Reach a surfaced road and turn right. In 50m fork left by a house, as the road loses its surface. Continue along a bramble-fringed lane. The track crosses a large area of marsh to head for a cut through the dunes/sea defences. To visit the beach, go through the gap; the vast stretch of sand, pounded by surf, stretches as far as the eye can see.

Return to the path and turn right (north). A good track stays parallel with the sea for about a mile (1.5km) to reach an informal National Trust car park. Turn left here to follow the access lane, initially between high hedgerows, back to the public road. For refreshments, turn left for 150m to the Poppylands tea shop.

Otherwise, turn right to follow the road round a left-hand bend and, in

100m, turn left at a 'Public Footpath' fingerpost to follow a narrow but clear path between fields. At the first hedge turn right at a junction, along a path leading to a few houses, Horsey Corner. Join a surfaced road, turning right then left in less than 10yds/m, at another 'Public Footpath' fingerpost. Continue over a bridge to a waymarked stile then go left along the top of a low embankment, soon bending to the right to head for a former mill – the Brograve Drainage Mill.

Just before the mill, go over a waymarked stile and up the side of an embankment, bearing left by the side of Waxham New Cut, with willowherb and tall marsh grass on either side of the path. Partway along this section, for environmental/ecological reasons the path has been diverted a short distance away from the waterway; follow the white disc markers as advised.

Horsey Mill is soon in view. Go over a stile and cross an open meadow, heading for a white disc on the far side. Go over a stile and up a few steps to take the obvious route to the mill, passing boat moorings on the final section.

Cycle Rides

Flat country, with numerous attractive destinations and a fair number of quiet lanes, adds up to a good recipe for cyclists. Inevitably many of the routes are roundabout but, for touring by cycle, arguably this is a plus rather than a minus. A good example is a circuit of 33 miles (53km) from Horning, visiting Ludham, Catfield, Hickling Green, Sutton Mill, East Ruston, Dilham, returning via the west side of Barton Broad, through Barton Turf and Nea-tishead to Horning.

Cycle hire is widely available throughout the area. Two suggestions:

Broadland Cycle Hire, Camelot Craft, The Rhond, Hoveton. ☎ 01603 783096.

Broads Bike Hire, Ludham Bridge. (with recommended long and short trails). ☎ (summer) 01603 782281, (winter) 01603 610734.

Car Tours

On a fine day the north Norfolk coast (see Chapters 1 and 2) beckons, with Hunstanton, Blakeney, Wells, Sheringham and Cromer all well with reach from any base in this area. For a different coastal experience, the comparatively undeveloped Suffolk coast to the south can be visited. On this coast, the vanished town of Dunwich and the attractive little towns of Southwold and Aldeburgh make fine excursions of a modest distance. For those more technologically minded, the Sizewell nuclear power station has a visitor centre and guided tours of parts of the plant.

Inland Suffolk is noted for its small towns and villages, often dominated by large and beautiful churches, typified by Lavenham and Long Melford. Bury St Edmunds, with cathedral, abbey ruins and much more to see, is the largest town and a focal point.

Places to Visit

Norwich

Norwich Castle Museum   *W*

☎ 01603 493636
Rotunda Coffee Shop. Provision for disabled visitors, including wheelchair and lift
Open daily, Mon to Sat 10am–4.30pm, Sun 1–5pm.

Origins at the Forum   *W*

☎ 01603 727920
An interactive journey through 2,000 years of life in Norfolk and Norwich
Open daily, Mon to Sat 10am–5.15pm, Sun 11am–4.45pm.

Inspire Discovery Centre   *W*

St Michael's Church, Coslany Street
☎ 01603 612612
Gift shop and basic refreshments
Open Mon to Fri 10am–5pm, Sat and Sun 11am–5pm.

Dragon Hall   *W*

115–121 King Street
☎ 01603 663922
A unique legacy of medieval life. Most of the exhibition is accessible to people with disabilities
Open Apr to Dec, Mon to Sat 10am–5pm. Closed from just before Christmas to the beginning of Jan.

Strangers' Hall   *V*

☎ 01603 667229
Home to merchants and mayors since 1320.
Open Weds and Sats, 10.30am–4.30pm.

The Bridewell   *W*

A former prison, now home to a collection of historic objects depicting historic domestic and business life in Norwich.
Open daily, Apr to Oct, Tue to Fri 10am–4.30pm (school terms closed Sun and Mon); 10am–5pm (school half-terms, Easter and summer holidays, closed Suns).

The Mustard Shop   *W*

Royal Arcade
Open during shop hours.

Sainsbury Centre for Visual Arts   *W*

University of East Anglia
☎ 01603 593199
Coffee bar. Facilities for the disabled, including electric wheelchair.
Open (summer season) from Tue to Sun 11am–5pm (Weds open until 8pm).

City of Norwich Aviation Museum   *W*

Horsham St Faith
☎ 01603 893080
Souvenir shop and tea room
Open beginning of Apr to end of Oct, Tue to Sat 10am–5pm, Suns and Bank Holidays 12–5pm; Nov to Mar, Weds and Sats 10am–4pm.

City Boats, River and Broads Cruises

☎ 01603 701701

Guided Walking Tours

Enquire at TIC, The Forum
☎ 01603 727927

Norwich Playhouse   *W*

☎ 01603 612580

Madder Market Theatre   *W*

☎ 01603 620917

Brundall to Stalham

Strumpshaw Steam Museum *W*

near Brundall
☎ 01603 714535
Refreshments and shop
Open Jun to Sep, Sun to Fri 11am–4pm. More restricted opening during Apr, May and Oct.

Bure Valley Railway

Wroxham
See Aylsham in Chapter 2.

Wroxham Barns *W*

☎ 01603 783762
Rural craft centre. Junior farm. Children's fairground. Tea rooms. Shops. Facilities for the disabled
Open every day except Christmas Day and Boxing Day, 10am–5pm. Fair is seasonal, 11am–5pm.

Hoveton Hall Gardens

☎ 01603 782798
Old Milking Parlour tea room
Open Easter Sun to early Sep, Wed, Fri, Sun and Bank Holiday Mons, 10am–5pm.

Royal Air Force Air Defence Radar Museum *W*

near Horning
☎ 01692 631485
Housed in the original 1942 Operations Building at RAF Neatishead. Exhibition includes a Battle of Britain Operations Room
Open on the second Sat of each month, Bank Holiday Mons and every Tue and Thu from Apr to Oct, 10am–5pm.

Toad Hall Cottage

How Hill, Ludham
☎ 01692 678763
Boat excursions and walking trails. Information; maps and souvenirs for sale
Open Jun to Sep, daily 9.30am–6pm; Apr, May and Oct, Mon to Fri 10.30am–1pm and 1.30–5pm, Sat and Sun 10.30am–5pm.

Museum of the Broads *W*

Stalham Staithe
☎ 01692 581681
Exhibitions of traditional Broadland craft and life. Shop
Open daily from Apr to Oct, 10.30am–5pm.

East Ruston Old Vicarage *W*

☎ 01692 650432
A 30-acre (12-hectare) coastal garden situated between Stalham and Happisburgh
Open late Mar to late Oct, Wed, Fri, Sat, Sun and Bank Holiday Mons, 2–5.30pm.

Waxham Barns *W*

Waxham Road, Sea Palling
Historic great barn with audio tour and tea rooms
Open from late Apr to late Oct, daily 10.30am–4.30pm (extended during school holidays).

Places to Visit

Sutton to Ranworth

Sutton Pottery *W*

near Stalham

☎ 01692 580595

Small working pottery

Open Mon to Fri 9am–1pm and 2–6pm.

Horsey Mill *W*

(National Trust)

☎ 01493 393904

Windpump. General stores with hot and cold drinks and ice cream. Open from late Mar to the end of Oct, daily (closed some Mons and Tues in Oct) 10am–4.30pm.

Hickling Broad Nature Reserve Visitor Centre

☎ 01692 598276

Shop, refreshments and toilets. Disabled access along the boardwalk and trail to the Broad. Boat trips in season (telephone for reservations) Open all year (nature reserve), Apr to mid-Sep (visitor centre), daily 10am–5pm

Caister Roman Fort

(English Heritage)

Open at all reasonable hours.

Caister Castle Car Collection *W*

☎ 01572 787251

Light refreshments, picnic area and disabled facilities

Open from the last week in May to the last Fri in Sep, daily except Sats 10am–4.30pm.

Norfolk Rare Breeds Centre *W*

Decoy House Farm, Ormesby St Michael

☎ 01493 732990

Open from early Jan to late Mar, Sun 11am–4pm; late Mar to the end of Oct, daily except Sat 11am–5pm; Nov and Dec, Sun 11am–4pm.

Thrigby Hall Wild Life Gardens

Thrigby Hall Wild Life Gardens

☎ 01493 369477
Café
Open every day of the year, 10am–5.30pm.

Fairhaven Woodland and Water Gardens

☎ 01603 270449
Restaurant, plant sales and gift shop
Open daily except Christmas Day, 10am–5pm (until 9pm, Weds and Thus, May to Aug).

Ranworth Broad Nature Reserve

☎ 0870 608 2608
Visitor Centre. Hot and cold drinks and ice cream
Open (visitor centre) from Apr to Oct, daily 10am–5pm.

Great Yarmouth

North West Tower

North Quay
Open from Jul to Sep, daily 10am–4pm.

Elizabethan House   *W*

4, South Quay
(National Trust)
☎ 01493 855746
Open early Apr to Oct, Mon to Fri 10am–5pm, Sat and Sun 1.15–5pm.

Old Merchant's House/Row 111 House   *W*

(English Heritage)
☎ 01493 857900
Open from the beginning of Apr to Sep, daily 12–5pm.

Greyfriars Cloisters   *W*

☎ 01493 857900
Open for guided tours only, Apr to Oct, first Wed of each month.

Maritime Museum

Marine Parade
☎ 01493 842267
Open during Easter and early holidays, Mon to Fri 10am–5pm, Sun 2–5pm; late May to late Sep, daily except Sat 10am–5pm.

Norfolk Nelson Museum   *W*

South Quay
☎ 01493 850698
Open daily, Apr to Oct, Mon to Fri 10am–5pm, Sat and Sun 1–4pm.

The Tolhouse   *W*

Tolhouse Street, off South Quay
☎ 01493 858900
Open Apr to Oct, Mon to Fri 10am–5pm, Sat and Sun 1.15–5pm.

Time and Tide   *W*

Blackfriars Road
☎ 01493 743930
Open Apr to Oct, daily 10am–5pm; Nov to Mar, Mon to Fri 10am–4pm, Sat and Sun 12–4pm.

Historic Smokehouse Museum and Great Yarmouth Potteries   *W*

Trinity Place/Blackfriars Road
☎ 01493 850585
Open all year, Mon to Fri 9.30am–2pm.
Composite tickets are available for the various attractions on South Quay, allowing discounts at each.

Places to Visit

Model Village

Marine Parade
☎ 01493 842097
Open from Apr to Oct.

Amazonia, the World of Reptiles *W*

Central Seafront
☎ 01493 842202
Open daily from 10.00.

Pleasure Beach

Marine Parade
☎ 01493 844585.

Burgh Castle to Beccles

Burgh Castle/Church Farm

Tea room at farm (Easter to Oct)
Castle open at any reasonable time.

Fritton Lake Countryworld

☎ 01493 488288
Café and shop
Open every day from early Apr to late Sep, 10am–5.30pm; Oct, weekends only.

Redwings Horse Sanctuary

Caldecott Visitor Centre, near Fritton
☎ 0870 040 0033
More than 70 acres of paddocks. Gift shop, café.

Somerleyton Hall and Gardens *W*

☎ 0871 2224244
Tea rooms, picnic area
Open from Apr to Oct, 12–4pm (hall), 10am–5pm (gardens), Thus, Suns and Bank Holidays. Also Tues and Weds in Jul and Aug.

Herringfleet Smock Mill

Open only on occasional days throughout the year, weather permitting, 1-5pm.

St Olave's Priory

☎ 01493 488609
Open at any reasonable time.

Raveningham Gardens

☎ 01508 548480
Open for two weeks in Feb (for snowdrops) and from Easter to the end of Aug, Mon to Fri 11am–4pm, Bank Holiday Suns and Mons 2–5pm. Home-made teas on Bank Holiday weekends.

Berney Arms Windmill *W*

(English Heritage)
☎ 01493 700605
Open from beginning of Apr to beginning of Nov, daily 9am–5pm (closed from 1–2pm).

Beccles and District Museum *W*

Ballygate, Beccles
☎ 01502 715722
Open from the beginning of Apr to the end of Oct, Tue to Sun and Bank Holiday Mons 2.30–5pm.

Bungay Museum *W*

Council Offices, Broad Street, Bungay
☎ 01986 894463
Open Mon to Fri, 9am–1pm and 2–4.30pm.

Printing Museum, William Clowes Ltd *W*

Newgate, Beccles
☎ 01502 712884
Open from Jun to Aug, Mon to Fri 2–4.30pm.

Station 146 Control Tower

Seething Airfield
☎ 01508 550288
Refreshments available
Open from May to Oct, first Sun of each month, 10am–5pm.

Norfolk and Suffolk Aviation Museum *W*

Buckaroo Way, The Street, Flixton, near Bungay (off A143)
☎ 01986 896644
Collection includes 50 historic aircraft. Open Apr to Oct, Sun to Thu 10am–5pm; Nov to Mar, Tue, Wed and Sun 10am–4pm.

East Anglia Transport Museum *W*

Chapel Road, Carlton Colville, Lowestoft
☎ 01502 518459
History of road transport, including working exhibits of trams and buses

Open from Easter to the end of Sep, Wed afternoons, Suns and Bank Holidays. Also Sat afternoons from Jun and more frequently during school holidays.

Otter Trust, Earsham

☎ 01986 893470
Tea room and gift shop
Open Good Fri to Oct, daly 10.30am–6pm. Feeding times 12pm and 3pm.

Play Barn (children's activity centre) *W*

Poringland
☎ 01508 495526
Open Mon to Fri 9.30am–3.30pm, Sun, 10am–5pm.

Caister Castle Car Collection

4. Breckland and South Norfolk

'The Breckland' is probably less well known to visitors as a coherent part of East Anglia than almost anywhere else in this book. Geographically it occupies the south-western part of Norfolk and a little of north Suffolk. 'The Breckland' is a mixture of grassy heath, pine shelter belts and arable land. A 'breck' was an area of land temporarily cultivated but allowed to revert to heath when its fertility was exhausted. Although the underlay is chalk, Breckland is largely covered by windblown sand, with some areas of gravel and boulder clay.

Human occupation came early to the area because of the easily cultivated light soils; permanent settlement goes back at least six thousand years. As the soils are thin, productivity during medieval times was poor and some of the settlements which were situated furthest from the vital water supplies became deserted. However, large numbers of sheep ensured that the overall economy remained healthy. The large proportion of heathland led to the establishment of shooting estates in the eighteenth and nineteenth cen-

turies. As these estates declined, much of the land was bought by the Forestry Commission in the 1920s, the result being the large coniferous forests so evident today.

From prehistoric times there has been a tradition of grazing sheep in large numbers on the open heaths which once covered most of Breckland. In addition, rabbits were introduced by the Normans for their meat and fur, in large warrens surrounded by earthen boundary banks, many still being visible in the pine forest. The soil erosion consequent

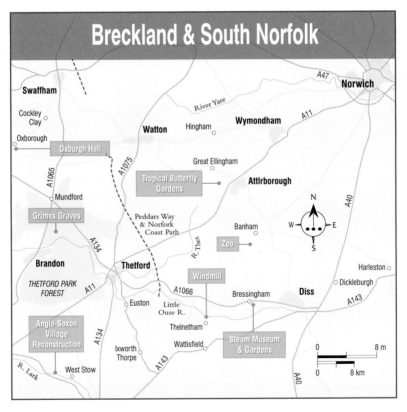

Breckland & South Norfolk

upon this intensive grazing resulted in periodic sand blows, contributing to a generally bleak, dry, countryside. The extraction of flint from the chalk for tools and weapons has been carried out for thousands of years. More recently flint has been a prime building material in East Anglia generally, often best seen in the numerous fine churches.

This unique combination of geology, previous land use and a drier, more continental, type of climate than is usual in Britain, has resulted in an unusual and surprisingly rich range of plants and animals.

This chapter also includes a part of South Norfolk to the south and south-west of Norwich, with pleasant small towns dotted throughout a generally agricultural countryside.

Thetford

The most important town of the area and a good place to start is **Thetford,** at the southern end of Breckland, by the confluence of the rivers Thet and Little Ouse, once one of the largest towns in the country. As long ago as the ninth century it was created the capital of a large area invaded by the Danes and was the See of the Bishops of East Anglia until 1091. Although those great days are long past, Thetford is still a busy market town and a centre for a large rural area.

Evidence of former greatness is provided by the remains of a twelfth-century Cluniac Priory, which is only one of a number of religious ruins, and **Castle Hill**, where Iron Age earthworks later had a Norman motte and bailey castle superimposed. Castle Hill stands as the largest mound of its kind in East Anglia and in the whole of England only Silbury Hill in Wiltshire is higher. Nearly every street has its quota of medieval and Georgian buildings; notable is the fifteenth-century '**Ancient House**' in White Hart Street, now in use as a small museum of local history.

The town is the birthplace of Thomas Paine, the great revolutionary and author of *The Rights of Man*. His gilded bronze statue of 1964 stands outside the King's House. The **Charles Burrell Museum** is housed in the former painting shop of the famous company which manufactured steam engines and agricultural machinery in the town from 1770 to 1932. The exhibits include recreated workshops and products, working drawings, photographs and much more.

The modern shopping centre is modest but does include a pedestrianised area, linking to a river promenade, with markets on Tues and Sats. The railway station has services on the Norwich to Ely and Peterborough line, with connections to Cambridge, London, the Midlands and the North.

Around Thetford

To the west and north-west of the town, **Thetford Forest** is the overall name given to a large area of woodland, most of it owned and managed by Forest Enterprises. Tree planting started in 1922, with Scots pine predominant. Corsican pine has since taken over as the favoured species but there are also areas of broad-leaved trees and of heathland. Forest Enterprises is noted for a generally 'visitor friendly' attitude and public use and enjoyment of the forest is encouraged, with many car parking/picnic areas and numerous waymarked trails up to 3 miles (5km) in length. The forest was designated as a 'Forest Park' in May 1990. Wildlife includes four types of deer and a small population of our native and much threatened red squirrel.

High Lodge Forest Centre has comprehensive visitor facilities, including a play area, café, shop and information. Cycle hire is available nearby. The centre is reached via the Forest Drive, a toll road. **'Go Ape'** has been added to the attractions of this very popular forest centre. This comprises a complex system of walkways, rope ladders and much more, all high above the forest floor and demanding a fair standard of fitness from participants. **Thetford Warren Lodge**, situated quite close to the B1107 road through the forest, was built about 1400 by the Prior of Thetford for his warrener, the servant who looked after the commercially important rabbit warrens. Once a group of buildings stood here but there was a great deal of damage caused by fire in 1935.

On the far side of the forest from Thetford, **Brandon** is a rather ordinary small town. The **Brandon Heritage Centre** in George Street has displays of local history from the stone age, with emphasis on flint knapping, fur and forest industries. Railway services are similar to Thetford but a smaller number of trains stop at Brandon. Brandon Country Park is a small part of a former large estate, bought by the Forestry Commission in 1927 and now managed by Suffolk County Council. There is a visitor centre with displays

and a small shop. The grounds, including a mausoleum and a walled garden, are available to the public for strolling and for picnics.

Between Brandon and Mundford, still within the overall forest area, is an open expanse covered with the remains of Neolithic flint mines. **Grimes Graves** mines were first operational some five thousand years ago but were not rediscovered and excavated until the 1870s. Although of great historical importance, there is not much for the visitor to see without donning a hard hat and descending into the only pit open to the public, 30ft (10m) deep, with radiating galleries. The site is operated by English Heritage. **Weeting Castle,** near Brandon, is also operated by English Heritage. The ruins of a late-twelfth-century moated manor house are incorporated into an eighteenth-century landscaped park, with a domed brick ice house.

A few miles towards Swaffham along the A1065 a left turn leads to **Cockley Cley,** a small village with an inn and an important visitor centre which incorporates a farm museum and a reconstruction of an Iceni village as it is believed to have been at the time of Boudicca, the great warrior queen. A two-storey gate structure gives access to living huts, a corn store, a chariot house with contemporary chariots and several other buildings. The story of Roman occupation, Boudicca's rebellion and her final defeat in AD 69 is well set out. Included in the same overall site are a furnished medieval house and St Mary's Chapel, with seventh-century origins, incredibly used as a primitive dwelling until 1952. Below the present ground level are the remains of a Roman temple.

Oxburgh Hall is a close neighbour to the west of Cockley Cley. Owned by the National Trust, this lovely moated house of 1482 is set in extensive grounds which include a wilderness garden and woodland walks. Inside the house are atmospheric Victorian interiors, needlework by Mary, Queen of Scots, the armoury, and a sixteenth-century priest's hole. The views from the roof are recommended.

From Watton to Banham

Heading back towards Norwich, **Watton** sprawls along the B1108, hardly a visitor town but with a Wed market and an unusual clock tower dated 1679. The Wartime Museum, with very limited opening hours, tells the story of RAF Watton and the town from 1937 to 1945. Still further to the

east, **Hingham** is a very pretty large village with greens flanked by narrow streets and Georgian houses.

Continuing eastwards, **Wymondham** is a more substantial market town with the magnificent twin-towered abbey church as the greatest feature. Also rather special is the timber-framed octagonal market cross, housing the Tourist Information Centre, at one end of High Street, replacing a structure destroyed in the great fire of 1615. The oldest inn is the Green Dragon, late-fifteenth-century and well placed as a hostelry to serve Abbey visitors.

For many centuries the abbey church operated in two parts; the resident monks had the nave, the north aisle and the north-west tower, whilst the towns-people had the remainder. This curious arrangement was, inevitably, caused by a long-standing feud. The monastic east end of the great church has gone, but the remainder still offers a great deal to the visitor. Inside, the fifteenth-century

Above: Wymondham TIC
Right: Iceni Village
Below: Wymondham Abbey
Opposite: Banham Zoo

nave roof, the twentieth-century gold altar screen and the triptych behind the altar in the north aisle are all exceptional. The brothers who initiated Ketts' Rebellion in 1549 were both local men. Having rallied great numbers of peasants against the enclosure of previously common pasture land, they attacked and took the city of Norwich, holding it for some weeks until defeated by superior Government forces. Robert was hanged at Norwich, William at Wymondham. The oak tree beside which they rallied a large gathering of supporters still lives, with support, by the B1172 Wymondham to Hethersett road.

The **Bridewell** has a local heritage museum, with exhibits of prison life. Following official condemnation of the previous Elizabethan prison, this building housed an early 'model' prison from 1785. The shopping area includes a number of both antique and general shops, with a street market on Fridays. The railway station has been beautifully renovated and now serves two purposes. Its prosaic, everyday, use is to give access to trains for passengers on the Norwich, Ely and Peterborough line. Its other use is to house a railway museum, model railway collection, gift shop and the unusual '**Brief Encounter**' themed restaurant. The Wymondham to East Dereham railway line was finally closed in 1989. It has since been restored by a volunteer organisation and now operates as a visitor attraction, with trains running along 11 miles (18km) of line from a station located close to the Abbey. There are ambitious plans to extend to North Elmham and, eventually, to Fakenham.

Approached through the hamlet of Caistor St Edmund on the south side of the A47, the Norwich southern ring road, **Venta Icenorum** is 'Norfolk's forgotten town', a comprehensive former Roman town and capital. Almost square, surrounded by large earth banks which are all that remains above ground, the site was opened to the public as recently as 1993. There is plenty of information on site and a car park adjacent. Further south along the A140, **Forncett Steam Museum** has a collection of large stationary steam engines dating from the early days of steam, now brought back to working order, with occasional 'steaming days'.

Attleborough is a small market (Thu) town with an interesting church, St Mary's, which was formerly cruciform but has lost its chancel and its apse. The central tower remains and there is some Norman work. The late-fifteenth-century rood screen, with painted decoration and a loft, has fortunately survived the Reformation. Railway services call here on the Norwich to Ely and Peterborough line. On the far side of Attleborough, **Banham Zoo**, on the fringe of Banham village, has a collection of big cats, shire horses, birds of prey, monkey islands, a farmyard corner and fun for children with a choice of restaurants. In total, there are more than a thousand animals and birds on more than 30 acres (12 hectares) of landscaped parkland.

From Harleston to Euston Hall

Harleston is a busy commercial centre and market town (Wed) situated in the Waveney Valley, on the boundary between Norfolk and Suffolk, with a mellow old marketplace and a few Georgian houses. **King George's Hall** in Broad Street houses a local museum. The 110th Bomb Group Memorial Museum at **Dickleburgh**, just north of Diss, occupies the control tower of the World War II base from which the group flew B17 Flying Fortresses. Exhibits comprise photographs, personal stories and memorabilia.

Diss is the most important market town of the area, with an attractive situation on the edge of a six-acre mere or lake. The church dominates one end of the sloping Market Place, with a pedestrianised shopping street, Mere Street, leading from the top end to the mere. Tudor, Georgian and Victorian buildings, some of them, such as Dolphin House at the top of the Market Place, timber framed, jostle together in the town centre. Specialised shops can be found in 'yards' off St Nicholas Street, close to the church. As is usual in an old market town, the best features of the buildings can be seen only by looking above the present-day ground-floor facades. A small **museum** in the Market Place has changing displays of the history and prehistory of Diss and its area.

A little way along the A1066 Thetford road, Alan Bloom has created one of Norfolk's showpieces at **Bressingham**, a unique mixture of gardens and steam railway museum, enhanced by fire engines, a Victorian roundabout and other attractions. No fewer than three operational steam narrow-gauge railways compete for custom with the static display of mainline standard-gauge locomotives from several countries, including a huge 2-10-0 from Norway. Some of the narrow-gauge locomotives have their ancestry firmly based in the great quarries of North Wales. Alan Bloom's Dell Garden is quite beautiful and is bordered by Adrian Bloom's Foggy Bottom Garden. On the far side of the main complex is a two-acre plant centre.

Knettishall Heath Country Park is a fine area of Breckland heath and woodland, just over the boundary into Suffolk, by the Little Ouse River, with waymarked trails, car park, picnic area, information centre and toilets. The Peddars Way and the Angles Way meet here.

Almost back in Thetford, **Euston Hall** has been the home of the Dukes of Grafton for more than 300 years. Built in the 1660s by Lord Arlington, it was remodelled in the 1750s. Among the contents are portraits by Van Dyck, Lely and Stubbs, the court of King Charles II being particularly featured. The pleasure grounds are by John Evelyn and the park and temple are by William Kent. The seventeenth-century church in the grounds is in the style of Sir Christopher Wren.

Walks

The 'Angles Way' connects Breckland with Broadland, running for a total of 77 miles (124km), largely along the valley of the River Waveney, visiting Diss, Harleston, Bungay and Beccles. For the Peddars Way, which heads north from the junction with the Angles Way at Knettishall Heath, see Chapter 1.

Below: Oxburgh Hall
Left: Sculpture in Thetford Forest

Thetford Forest has no fewer than 24 generally easy waymarked walks up to a maximum length of 4 miles (6km), all related to car parking areas. At Lynford Arboretum there is an 'easy access trail' accessible to the disabled.

Cycle Rides

The Thetford Forest area is very appealing, using the lesser public roads, preferably in conjunction with specifically waymarked cycle routes within the forest, where the surfaced tracks are available to cyclists. Cycles can be hired at the High Lodge Forest Centre.

From the previously mentioned 'Norfolk Cycle Map', available from Tourist Information Centres, a 35-mile (55km) circuit based on the Upper Waveney Valley links Diss, Redgrave, Thelnetham, East Harling, New Buckenham, Gissing and Diss.

Car Tours

From a Breckland base, anywhere in East Anglia is reachable as a day excursion – just scan the chapters in this book and make your choice. In particular, Cambridge, with its manifest attractions, is within easy reach.

Public Transport

The Norwich to Peterborough railway line, with connections at Ely and Peterborough to Cambridge, London, the Midlands, Scotland and the North-East, passes through Breckland. There are stations at Wymondham, Attleborough, Harling Road, Thetford, Brandon and Mildenhall. The Norwich to Ipswich and London railway line passes through Diss.

'Sun Rover' tickets are available on many of the bus routes throughout Breckland and South Norfolk, involving towns and villages such as Thetford, Bressingham, Diss, Harleston, Poringland, Attleborough and Wymondham. For more information call Traveline (☎ 0870 608 2 608).

Places to Visit

Thetford to Oxburgh Hall

Thetford Priory

(English Heritage)
☎ 01604 730320
Open at any reasonable time.

Ancient House Museum   *W*

Thetford
☎ 01842 752599
Recently re-opened after major refurbishment.

Charles Burrell Museum   *W*

Thetford
☎ 01842 765840
Open from Apr to the end of Oct, Tue 10am–2pm, last Sat in month 10am–4pm.

High Lodge Forest Centre, Thetford Forest Park   *W*

☎ 01842 815434
Information, café and gift shop. Children's play area
Open all year from 9am, seasonal closing times. Charge for motor vehicles.

Go Ape at Thetford Forest

☎ 0870 458 9187
Advance booking required.

Brandon Forest Park and Visitor Centre

☎ 01842 810185
Gift shop with drinks and ice cream.

Brandon Heritage Centre   *W*

☎ 07709 236446
The story of Brandon from Neolithic times to the present day.

Open from Easter to Oct, weekends and Bank Holidays.

Grimes Graves

(English Heritage)
☎ 01842 810656
Open from Mar to Oct, 10am–5pm (6pm from Apr to Sep).

Weeting Castle

(English Heritage)
☎ 01604 730320
Ruins of medieval moated manor house.

Cockley Cley Iceni Village and Museums

(English Heritage)
☎ 01760 721339
Disabled access. Gift shop, tea room and toilets.
Open daily from beginning of Apr to end of Oct, 11am–5.30pm (opens at 10am during Jul and Aug).

Oxburgh Hall   *W*

(National Trust)
Shop and restaurant
Open from late Mar to the beginning of Nov, daily except Thu and Fri, 1–5pm (4pm in Oct); Bank Holiday Mons 11am–5pm. Gardens are also open in winter, Sats and Suns, 11am–4pm. Garden, shop and restaurant are open daily in Aug.

Gooderstone Water Gardens

near Oxborough
Six acres of garden, with nature trail, bird hide, tea room and plant sales
Open daily all year from 10am–6pm (or dusk if earlier).

Places to Visit

Watton to Banham

Wymondham Heritage Museum, The Bridewell   *W*

☎ 01953 600205
Gift shop and tea room
Open from the beginning of Mar to the end of Nov, Mon to Sat 10am–4pm, Sun 2–4pm.

Wymondham Station   *W*

☎ 01953 606433
Railway memorabilia, gift shop and refreshment room (The Brief Encounter).
Open daily, 10am–5pm (Sun 11.30am–5.30pm)
Note also the restored Mid-Norfolk Railway line to East Dereham (operating from its own station close to the abbey):
☎ 01362 690633.

Melsop Farm Park

Scoulton, near Watton
☎ 01953 851943
Small and large animals including rare breeds. Demonstrations, play area, gift shop and café.
Open Mar to the end of Oct, Tue to Sun, 10am–5pm; also weekends and school holidays, Nov to Feb.

Venta Icenorum

☎ (TIC) 01953 604721
Open at all reasonable times.

Banham Zoo   *W*

☎ 01953 887771
Children's play area. Crafts and shops complex with pub and other refreshments.
Open daily from 10am – seasonal closing times.

Harleston to Euston Hall

Harleston Museum   *W*

Open from early May to late Oct, Weds 10am–noon and 2–4pm, Sats 10am–noon.

Diss Museum   *W*

☎ 01379 650618
Open all year, Wed and Thu 2–4pm, Fri and Sat 10.30am–4.30pm. Closed during Christmas and New Year.

100ᵗʰ Bomb Group Memorial Museum

Dickleburgh
☎ 01379 740708
Open Sats, Suns and Bank Holidays throughout the year, 10am–5pm (closed Nov, Dec and Jan); May to Sep, also Weds 10am–5pm.

Bressingham Steam Museum Trust and Gardens

☎ 01379 686900
Shop, garden shop and café
Open daily, 10.30am–5.30pm.

Euston Hall   *W*

☎ 01842 766366
Old Kitchen tea shop, picnic area and craft shop. Wheelchair access to tea room, craft shop and grounds only
Hall open on Thus from early Jun to late Sep and on occasional Sundays, afternoons only.

Accommodation

Throughout the area covered in this book, accommodation is available to suit all needs and budgets – from the ultimate in luxury hotels, secluded country hotels, lodges for travellers, hospitable pubs, bed and breakfast in private houses, farm accommodation, self-catering cottages and apartments from basic to de luxe, youth hostels and bunkhouses. Particularly in the larger hotels, huge variations in tariff can occur, with many special offers available for out of season breaks, midweek or weekend bargains; it is well worth shopping around. If calling personally at any establishment prior to making a reservation, it is quite acceptable to ask to see the available room.

Whilst some of the establishments listed are known to the authors, the inclusion in this book does not necessarily constitute a recommendation.

The listings below provide a sample of accommodation and restaurants available; more extensive lists may be obtained from the relevant Tourist Information Centre where, in the majority of cases, a reservation service is provided.

A summary of the main types of accommodation is given below:

Major and large hotels
Throughout the area there are many highly rated hotels. Most offer all the services expected of an international hotel. In addition to the main restaurant, less formal eating areas such as the bar will offer meals and room service is usually available. Swimming pools and gymnasium facilities are often provided in hotels of this standard; most will cater for conferences.

Country house hotels
These are usually large houses in extensive grounds. Architecture and decor is frequently de luxe and service is attentive. Such hotels usually have a tranquil setting and are intended to provide the guests with a caring and relaxing environment. It is customary to reserve a room, breakfast and evening meal at this type of hotel ('half board').

Small hotels and guest houses
These are more modest establishments, normally with fewer facilities than the large hotels. Whilst most will have bathrooms or shower rooms en suite, not all will have telephones in each bedroom and evening meals may not be available.

Bed and Breakfast
This is accommodation offered in private houses or small proprietor-run guest houses in towns, villages or rural areas. Standards will vary and this usually reflected in the price. Look for the B & B sign outside – some will quote the price; otherwise enquire at the door. Most offer at least some rooms with en-suite facilities. The majority do not serve meals other than breakfast but will suggest local restaurants and pubs to suit all budgets. Some of these properties will have a residents' lounge; almost all will provide tea and coffee facilities and television in the bedrooms. Remember, you can ask to see the room offered before accepting the accommodation.

Farmhouse accommodation
Generally similar to the bed and breakfast described above but situated in houses attached to working farms. Find addresses from TICs or specialised guidebooks. Again standards will vary from simple to quite luxurious. Evening meals, if available, will sometimes be taken round a large table with the family and other guests. Some farmers will welcome guests to look round the farm and perhaps encourage them to help with the feeding of livestock.

Self-catering – cottages, apartments and residential caravans
There are agents who will offer a choice of property to rent, usually on a weekly basis but sometimes for shorter periods. The size of the property, its facilities and the rent will vary considerably; most are considerably cheaper out of the main holiday season. It is also possible to rent properties directly from the owner; these are advertised in the weekend newspapers and in magazines such as *The Lady*; many are listed in booklets obtainable from Tourist Information Centres.

Some agencies offering self-catering accommodation:

North Norfolk Holiday Homes
130 properties throughout the area, ☎ 01328 855322

Norfolk Country Cousins
90 properties, ☎ (Freephone) 0500 400 407

Norfolk Country Cottages
good selection of properties available, ☎ 01603 871872

Suffolk and Norfolk Country Cottages
many properties available, ☎ 01359 271350

Russells Self-Catering Holidays
variety of accommodation available close to Norfolk coast, ☎ 01263 513139

Camping and caravan sites

Generally, sites open only from mid-March to mid-November but there are exceptions. Some sites have large static caravans and/or timber chalets to rent on a weekly (sometimes shorter) basis, bringing them into the category above. Some sites will cater for the full range of touring caravans, motor caravans and tents, whilst others will be restricted to either caravans/motor caravans or tents. Farmers sometimes hold a local authority license to use a small field for tents. The larger caravan and campsites are well equipped with showers, laundry, dish-washing sinks and other facilities. Lists of sites can be obtained from Tourist Information Centres.

The two major clubs, the Caravan Club and the Camping and Caravanning Club, own and manage sites in the area. Whilst the Caravan Club is predominantly for touring caravans, some of its sites do take tents. Some Club sites are provided for members only but those listed in this guide are available both to members and non-members; the latter will pay a slightly increased overnight fee. The small 'certified location' sites licensed by the Clubs are for members only and are limited to five vans per night; this type of site is frequently found to be a small field on a working farm; many do not have electrical hook-ups or toilet facilities.

Details of membership, possible reciprocal arrangements with clubs in other countries and further information may be obtained from:

The Caravan Club
East Grinstead House, East Grinstead, RG19 1UA, ☎ 01342 326944, www.caravanclub.co.uk

The Camping and Caravanning Club
Greenfield House, Westwood Way, Coventry, CV4 8JH, ☎ 01203 694995
www.campingandcaravanningclub.co.uk

A Camping International Card, obtainable from camping and caravan clubs in many countries, may be useful.

Youth Hostels

There are several hostels in the area covered by this guide, established in a wide variety of buildings, some in cities and large towns, some in quiet rural areas. It must be emphasised that, despite the name, hostels are for all travellers: young, not-so-young, solo, groups, school parties, families – all are welcome. Booking ahead is advisable but not always essential.

Youth Hostels Association
Trevelyan House, Dimple Road, Matlock, Derbyshire, DE4 3YH
☎ 0870 770 8868 or 01629 592700, www.yha.org.uk
Membership includes a copy of the handbook listing details of all the hostels in England and Wales, with the facilities offered and a location map. The accommodation includes both family rooms and dormitories. Bed linen is provided and its use is included in the modest overnight charge. Hostels usually provide meals, sometimes with a choice of menu, and always a vegetarian option. Other diets can be catered for subject to advance notice. Charges for meals are reasonable and local produce is usually used. All hostels provide facilities for those preferring self-catering. Some hostels have a closed period during the day, usually 10am–5pm. Note also that not all hostels are open all the year, some being available on a rent-a-hostel basis.
Youth Hostels within the area covered by this guide are:

Great Yarmouth – just out of town centre. ☎ 0870 770 5840

Hunstanton – Avenue Road. ☎ 0870 770 5872

King's Lynn – near the quay. ☎ 0870 770 5902

Sheringham – Cremer's Drift. ☎ 0870 770 6024

Wells-next-the-Sea – Church Plain. ☎ 0870 770 6084

Accommodation and Eating Out

(arranged in accordance with the chapters in the main guide)

King's Lynn and North-West Norfolk

Hotels

King's Lynn
The Duke's Head – 71 rooms, ☎ 01553 774996.

Knight's Hill Hotel
Near King's Lynn
South Wootton – 77 rooms, ☎ 01553 675566

Ramada Hotel
Near King's Lynn
A modern hotel with 50 rooms, ☎ 01553 771707

Congham Hall Country House Hotel
Grimston near King's Lynn
luxury hotel. ☎ 01485 600250

The Hoste Arms
Burnham Market – 35 rooms, ☎ 01328 738777

The George Hotel
Swaffham – 29 rooms, ☎ 01760 721238

Stratton House
near the Market Place – 10 rooms
In town centre but country house style hotel.
☎ 01760 723845

Hunstanton
The Linksway Country House Hotel, Old
Hunstanton – 14 rooms, ☎ 01485 532209

Guest Houses and similar establishments

The Old Rectory
King's Lynn, 33 Goodwins Road
☎ 01553 768544

Marsh Farm
Wolferton near King's Lynn, ☎ 01485 540265

Self-catering

Belle Vue Apartments
Hunstanton
☎ 01485 532826 (day) ☎ 532156 (eve)

Hall Barn Cottages
Near Swaffham
Beachamwell, ☎ 01366 328794

Caravan and Camping Sites

Sandringham Estate Caravan Site
Sandringham. no tents. ☎ 01553 631614

Pentney Park Caravan Site
Near King's Lynn
Narborough – Touring caravans, motor homes
and tents, ☎ 01760 337479

Restaurants/Tea shops

The Orangery
Grimston, near King's Lynn
Congham Hall – award-winning restaurant
☎ 01485 600250

The Hoste Arms
Burnham Market
restaurant – also bar meals, ☎ 01328 738777

Willow Cottage Tea Rooms
Castle Acre, ☎ 01760 755551

The restaurant/tea room at the visitor centre
Sandringham

The Mill tea room
Great Bircham

Sheringham, Cromer and North-East Norfolk

Hotels

The Blakeney Hotel
Blakeney, 64 rooms, ☎ 01263 740797

Wensum Lodge Hotel
Fakenham
very near to town centre – 17 rooms
☎ 01328 862100

The Crown Hotel
Wells-next-the-Sea
12 rooms, ☎ 01328 710209

Elderton Lodge Hotel and Restaurant
Near Cromer, Thorpe Market
11 rooms, ☎ 01263 833547

Buckinghamshire Arms
Blickling
traditional inn adjacent to Blickling Hall –
3 rooms, ☎ 01263 732133

Caravan and Camping Sites

The Race Course Caravan Site
Fakenham, ☎ 01328 862388

Brick Kilns Caravan Site
Near Fakenham
Barney (5 miles from Fakenham)
☎ 01328 878305

Little Haven Camping and Caravan Park
Aylsham, Erpingham, ☎ 01263 768959

Restaurants/Tea shops

The Old Stable Restaurant
Fakenham
lunches and dinners, ☎ 01328 855947

The Owl Tea Rooms
Holt, ☎ 01263 713232

*The Old Bakehouse Tea Room and
Guest House*
Little Walsingham, ☎ 01328 820454

Norwich and
the Norfolk Broads

Hotels

The Holiday Inn
Norwich
Ipswich Road – 116 rooms, ☎ 08704 009060

Dunston Hall Hotel
4 miles from Norwich
luxury hotel in 110 acres – 170 rooms
☎ 01508 470444

Park Farm Country Hotel
Hethersett – 42 rooms
set in landscaped gardens, ☎ 01603 810264

Self-catering

Spixworth Hall Cottages
Norwich
8 properties, ☎ 01603 898190

Premier Marina Cottages
Horning
20 properties, ☎ 01692 630392

Poppyland Holiday Cottages
Overstrand – 6 properties ☎ 01263 577473

Three cottages at Hardley near Loddon
☎ 01371 850853

Caravan and Camping Sites

Caravan Club Site
Great Yarmouth – no tents, ☎ 01493 855223

Norfolk Showground Caravan Club Site
Norwich, ☎ 01603 742708

Bureside Holiday Park
Acle
Touring caravans, motor homes and tents
☎ 01493 369233

Swans Harbour Caravan Park
Near Norwich, Marlingford, ☎ 01603 759658

Restaurants/Tea shops

Cathedral Restaurant
Norwich, closed Sundays, ☎ 01603 471066

*Jarrolds Department Store in the centre
has a choice of three restaurants.*

The Old Barn Tea Rooms at Wroxham
Barns Craft Centre

Alfresco tea room
Ludham
light lunches and teas, ☎ 01692 678384

Breckland and South Norfolk

Hotels

Wymondham Consort Hotel
Wymondham, 12 rooms, ☎ 01953 606721

The Abbey Hotel
29 rooms, ☎ 01953 602148

The Thomas Paine Hotel
Thetford, 12 rooms, ☎ 01842 755631

Broom Hall Country Hotel
Near Thetford
Saham Toney – 15 rooms, ☎ 01953 882125

The Half-Moon Inn
Near Diss, Rushall – 10 rooms, ☎ 01379 740793

Self-catering

Coach and Pump Cottage
Diss, The Hayloft and The Olde Laundry
– four cottages, ☎ 01379 668146

Caravan and Camping Sites

Puddledock Farm
Near Thetford, Great Hockham
☎ 01953 498455

The Covert Caravan Club Site
between Thetford and Swaffham (no toilet
facilities), ☎ 01842 878356

Lowe Caravan Park
Saham Hills, Watton
Touring caravans, motor homes, holiday caravans
for hire, ☎ 01953 881051

Restaurants/Tea shops

The restaurant at Bressingham Gardens
Bressingham

'Brief Encounter'
Wymondham
at the station – working station but some
buildings converted into museum and intriguing
restaurant – well worth a visit for something out
of the ordinary.

The Tea Room
Thetford Forest Visitor Centre

Leisure, Activities and Events

(arranged in accordance with the chapters in the main guide)

King's Lynn and North-West Norfolk

Sports Centres

King's Lynn Sports and Leisure Centre
Green Park Avenue, King's Lynn
☎ 01553 818001

Oasis Leisure Centre
Hunstanton, ☎ 01485 534227

Swimming Pools

Dereham
Quebec Road, ☎ 01362 693419

Oasis Leisure
Hunstanton, ☎ 01485 534227

St James Swimming Pool
Blackfriars Street
King's Lynn, ☎ 01553 764888

Golf

Middleton Hall
near King's Lynn, ☎ 01553 841800

King's Lynn
Castle Rising, ☎ 01553 631227

Eagles Golf Centre
School Road, Tilney All Saints,
near King's Lynn, ☎ 01553 827147

Dereham Golf Club
☎ 01362 695900

Swaffham Golf Club
☎ 01760 721611

Fakenham Golf Club
☎ 01328 863534

Royal West Norfolk
Brancaster, ☎ 01485 210223

Dunham Golf Club
near Swaffham, ☎ 01328 701718

Horse Riding

Riding stables are widespread throughout the county; see appropriate yellow pages or enquire at tourist information centres.

Sailing/Windsurfing

Leziate Park Sailing and Social Club
Brow of the Hill, Leziate, ☎ 01553 630393

Hunstanton Sailing Club
The Promenade, ☎ 01485 534705

Angling

Narborough Trout Lakes, not far from King's Lynn, have fully organised fishing for coarse fish and for trout. Facilities for the disabled, shop, refreshments and picnic area are available. ☎ 01760 338005
Sea fishing is possible from numerous sandy beaches.

Events

Traditional King's Lynn May Garland Procession
Beginning of May, ☎ 01553 768930

The Original King's Lynn Fleamarket
Mid-May, mid-July and mid-November
☎ 01485 541566

King's Lynn Country Music Festival
Late May, ☎ 01366 387440

Spring Spectacular
Sandringham
Late May, ☎ 01553 772675.

Hunstanton and District Festival of Arts
Mid to late June, ☎ 01485 540950.

Hunstanton Carnival
Late June, ☎ 01485 525410.

County Tennis Week
Hunstanton
Late July, ☎ 01485 532516, ext. 3211.

King's Lynn Festival of Music and the Arts
Late July, ☎ 01553 773578.

King's Lynn Festival Too
Street entertainment and evening concerts
Late July and early August
☎ 01553 761188.

Hunstanton Gala Day
Late August, ☎ 01485 532610.

Sheringham, Cromer and North-East Norfolk

Sports Centres

Aylsham Multi Sports Area
Aylsham High School
Includes swimming pool, ☎ 01603 703266

Cromer Sports Hall
Cromer High School, ☎ 01263 515669

North Walsham Sports Hall
☎ 01692 402293

Reepham Sports Club
Includes swimming pool, ☎ 01603 870969

Swimming Pools

The Splash
Sheringham
Includes leisure pool and wave pool
☎ 01263 825675

See also 'Sports Centres' above.

Golf

Royal Cromer Golf Club
☎ 01263 512884.

Sheringham Golf Club
☎ 01263 823488.

West Runton Links Country Park Golf Club
☎ 01263 838383

Mundesley Golf Club
☎ 01263 720279

Mattishall Golf Club
☎ 01362 850111

Wensum Valley Golf Club
Taverham, ☎ 01603 261012

Angling

Freshwater – there is great potential in this area; for details of licences contact the Environment Agency (Anglian Region): ☎ 08708 506 506; or buy your licence over the phone on ☎ 0870 1662 662.

Felbrigg Hall Lake
☎ 01263 513676

Gunton Lake

Gunthorpe Hall Lake
☎ 01263 861373

Blickling Lake
Sea – numerous sandy beaches: Cromer, West Runton, Sheringham, Weybourne, Salthouse and Cley, Eccles and Cart Gap, Walcott and Bacton, Mundesley and Trimingham and Overstrand are all popular, ☎ 01263 734181

Trout and land-locked salmon
Bure Valley Lakes
☎ 01263 587666

Events

See National Trust and English Heritage annual leaflets. 'Carnivals and Festivals' in the *Norfolk Coast Guardian* free annual newspaper, available at Tourist Information Centres.

Norwich and the Norfolk Broads

Golf

Costessey Park Golf Course
Norwich ☎ 01603 746333

Great Yarmouth and Caister Golf Club
☎ 01493 720421

Eaton Golf Club
☎ 01603 51686

Royal Norwich Golf Club
☎ 01603 429928

Caldecott Hall Golf Club
near Gt. Yarmouth, ☎ 01493 488488

Bawburgh Golf Club
near Norwich, ☎ 01603 740404

Barnham Broome Golf and Country Club
☎ 01603 759393

Sprowston Park Golf Club
☎ 01603 410657

Sports Centres

Broadland Sports Club
Main Road, Fleggburgh, ☎ 01493 369651

Marina Leisure Centre
Great Yarmouth, ☎ 01493 851521

Norman Centre
Norwich, ☎ 01603 408140

Norwich Sports Village
☎ 01603 788898

Sprowston Sports Hall
Norwich, ☎ 01603 703266

Stalham Sports Hall
The High School, ☎ 01692 580864

Sports Park at UEA
Norwich, ☎ 01603 592399

Wensum Lodge
Norwich, ☎ 01603 624326

Swimming Pools

Several of the above sports centres, plus:

Broadland Aquapark
Hellesdon, Norwich, ☎ 01603 788912

Fitness Express
Barnham Broom, ☎ 01603 759741

Hoveton Swimming Pool
☎ 01603 782715

Phoenix Pool
off Mallard Way, Bradwell, Great Yarmouth
☎ 01493 664575

St Augustine's Swimming Centre
Norwich, ☎ 01603 620164

Waveney River Centre
Burgh St Peter, near Beccles, ☎ 01502 677343

Sailing/windsurfing

Fritton Lake
Fritton, Great Yarmouth, ☎ 01493 488378

Fishing Trips

M. Dyble
Great Yarmouth, ☎ 01493 731305

Bishop Boat Services
Great Yarmouth, ☎ 01493 664739

M. Rea
Great Yarmouth, ☎ 01493 859653

Horse Racing

Great Yarmouth Racecourse
☎ 01493 720343

Motor Sports

Yarmouth Stadium
Stock cars, bangers, hot rods
☎ 01493 720343

Boat Hire

Most of the major and some minor boating centres have boatyards from which motor cruisers and day boats can be hired. A smaller number also have sailing boats. The following is a sample:

City Boats
Norwich. ☎ 01603 701701

Wroxham Launch Hire
☎ 01603 783043

Broads Tours
Wroxham and Potter Heigham
☎ 01603 782207 or 01692 670711

George Smith and Sons
Wroxham, ☎ 01603 782527

Blakes Holidays Ltd.
Wroxham, ☎ 01603 784458

Broads Tours Ltd.
Wroxham, ☎ 01603 782207

Broom Boats Ltd. Riverside
Brundall, ☎ 01603 714803

Highcraft
Griffin Lane, Thorpe St Andrew
Norwich, ☎ 01603 701701

Norfolk Broads Yachting Co. Ltd.
Lower Street, Horning, ☎ 01692 631330

River Craft
The Staithe, Stalham, ☎ 01692 580288

Herbert Woods
Broads Haven, Potter Heigham
☎ 01692 670711

Excursion boats operate from Wroxham, Horning, Norwich, Stalham and Oulton Broad.

Events

Great Yarmouth Races. Several meetings each month throughout the summer.

Caister Carnival
Late June.

Royal Norfolk Show
Early July.

Martham Carnival
Early July.

Beccles Carnival
End of July/beginning of August.

Stalham Carnival
Early August.

Great Yarmouth Carnival Week
with procession. Mid-August.

Filby Fun Weekend
Late August.

Norfolk and Norwich Festival
Mid-October.

Breckland and South Norfolk

Golf

Thetford Golf Club
☎ 01842 752169

Diss Golf Club
☎ 01493 661911

Richmond Park Golf Club
near Watton, ☎ 01953 881803

Reymaston Golf Cub
near Hingham, ☎ 01362 850297

Sports Centres

Waterworld
Breckland Leisure Centre, Thetford
☎ 01842 753110

Attleborough Sports Hall
☎ 01953 454116

Breckland Leisure Centre
Thetford, ☎ 01842 753110

Hingham Sports Hall
Watton Road, Hingham, ☎ 01953 850953

Harleston Leisure Centre
☎ 01379 852088

Long Stratton Leisure Centre
☎ 01508 531444

Wymondham Leisure Centre
☎ 01953 607171

Swimming Pools

Diss Swimming Pool
☎ 01379 652754

Fishing
Organised fisheries include:

Woodrising Carp Fishery
Cranworth, ☎ 01362 820702

Scoulton Mere
☎ 01603 811003

Whinburgh Trout Lake
☎ 01362 850201

Buckenham Pits
☎ 01842 878395

Thompson Water Fishery
☎ 01953 882942

Middle Harling Lake
☎ 01953 717909

Loch Neaton Fishery
Watton, ☎ 01953 881760

Hingham Carp Fishery
☎ 01953 850308: Walnut Farm Fisheries (canal and lake), ☎ 01953 455282

Balloon flights

Breckland Balloons
East Dereham, ☎ 01362 691305

Events

Thetford Forest Park
Activity days throughout the season. Plays and musical events in summer

Wymondham Music Week
June, ☎ 01508 533681

Mildenhall Air Fete
late May

Weeting Steam Rally
mid-July

Airports
Norwich Airport. ☎ 01603 411923

Car Hire
Enterprise Rent a Car. ☎ 01992 509990
Kenning Car and Van Rental. Several locations across East Anglia. ☎ 0541 55590
Willhire Ltd. ☎ 0345 161718

Naturalists' Organisations
Broads Authority, 18 Colegate, Norwich. ☎ 01603 610734
The National Trust, Blickling, Norwich. ☎ 01263 733471
Norfolk Wildlife Trust, 72 Cathedral Close, Norwich. ☎ 01603 625540
Royal Society for the Protection of Birds, Stalham House, 65 Thorpe Road, Norwich. ☎ 01603 661662
English Nature (Norfolk), 60 Brancondale, Norwich. ☎ 01603 620558
Norfolk Ornithologists' Association, Aslack Way, Holme next the Sea, Hunstanton, ☎ 01485 525406
Nature Reserves throughout East Anglia are too numerous to mention in total; lists are widely available in the area. The most important are included in the relevant chapters. Below are those operated by the Royal Society for the Protection of Birds:
Ouse Washes (see Chapter 1). ☎ 01354 680212
Snettisham, on the shore of the Wash. Large numbers of wading birds, ducks and geese, particularly as the tide is rising. ☎ 01485 542689
Titchwell Marsh, 5 miles (8km) east of Hunstanton. Wetland – reed beds and shallow lagoons. Ducks, geese and, in summer, the rare marsh harrier. ☎ 01485 210779.
Strumpshaw Fen, near to Brundall, in the heart of the Norfolk Broads. Reedbeds and woodland. Swallowtail butterflies. Many birds, including bearded tits. ☎ 01603 715191.
Surlingham Church Marsh, on the opposite side of the River Yare to Strumpshaw Fen, 6 miles (10km)

east of Norwich. Birds of reed and sedge fen, ditches and open water. ☎ 01508 538661.

Berney Marshes and Breydon Water, accessed from the Asda car park near Great Yarmouth railway station. Grazing marshes and mudflats. ☎ 01493 700645.

Guides

The Registered Blue Badge Guide Scheme applies throughout East Anglia. All such guides have attended an approved training scheme and can be identified when wearing the 'Blue Badge'. Some of the guides have a further qualification to conduct visitors, either individually or in groups on longer tours in the region. Lists of guides are obtainable from the East of England Tourist Board (☎ 0845 300 6996).

Established tours conducted by registered guides:

King's Lynn – regular town tours and group tours. Kings Lynn Town Guides, ☎ 01553 765714

Norwich – Regular city tours, evening tours, group tours and day or half-day group coach tours of Norfolk/East Anglia. Call Norwich TIC (☎ 01603 727927).

Walsingham – Walking guided tours. ☎ 01328 820250.

Maps

For the general visitor who likes to use a good map, there is nothing to beat the Ordnance Survey Landranger (red) series. Every town, every village, every road, both main and minor, every river, every stream, virtually every footpath; all are included, together with a wealth of extra information, much of it specifically directed at visitors. To the practised eye, the contour lines and other landscape features give a good overall picture of an area. The scale of these maps is 1:50,000; the following sheets cover the area included in this book:

No. 132 – North West Norfolk
No. 133 – North East Norfolk
No. 134 – Norwich and the Broads, Great Yarmouth
No. 143 – Ely and Wisbech, Downham Market
No. 144 – Thetford and Diss, Breckland and Wymondham

For more specialised requirements, the larger 1:25,000 scale of the Ordnance Survey Explorer series may be advantageous in its greater detail: Outdoor Leisure map no. 40 (The Broads) gives complete cover of the Norfolk and Suffolk Broads. The North Norfolk Coast is covered by three of the Explorer maps, Nos. 250, 251 and 252.

Tourist Information Centres

(* indicates seasonal opening)

Norfolk

*Attleborough, Queens Square
☎ 01953 456930
Aylsham, Bure Valley Railway Station, Norwich Road. ☎ 01263 733903
Burnham Deepdale, Deepdale Farms
☎ 01485 210256
Cromer, Bus Station, Prince of Wales Road
☎ 0871 200 3071
*Dereham, Church Street. ☎ 01362 698992
Diss, Meres Mouth, Mere Street.
☎ 01379 650523
Downham Market, Priory Centre.
☎ 01366 383287
*Great Yarmouth, Marine Parade.
☎ 01493 846345
Harleston, Exchange Street. ☎ 01379 851917
*Holt, Pound House. ☎ 0871 200 3071
*Hoveton, Station Road. ☎ 01603 782281
*How Hill, Toad Hole Cottage.
☎ 01692 678763
Hunstanton, Town Hall, The Green.
☎ 01485 532610

King's Lynn, Custom House.
☎ 01553 763044
*Loddon, The Old Town Hall.
☎ 01508 521028
*Mundesley, 2a, Station Road.
☎ 01263 721070
Norwich, The Forum. ☎ 01603 727927
*Potter Heigham, The Staithe.
☎ 01692 670779
*Ranworth, The Staithe. ☎ 01603 270453
*Sheringham, Station Approach.
☎ 0871 200 3071
*Stalham, Museum of the Broads.
☎ 01692 581681
*Swaffham, Market Place. ☎ 01760 722255
Thetford, White Hart Street. ☎ 01842 820689
*Walsingham, Shirehall Museum.
☎ 01328 820510
*Watton & Wayland, The Visitor Centre.
☎ 01953 880212
*Wells-next-the-Sea, Staithe Street.
☎ 0871 200 3071
Wymondham, Market Place.
☎ 01953 604721

Suffolk

*Beccles, The Quay, Fen Lane, ☎ 01502 713196

Index

Published in the UK by:
Landmark Publishing Ltd,
Ashbourne Hall, Cokayne Avenue, Ashbourne,
Derbyshire DE6 1EJ England
E-mail landmark@clara.net Website www.landmarkpublishing.co.uk

1st Edition

ISBN 13: 978-1-84306-327-8
ISBN 10: 1-84306-327-1

© **Norman & June Buckley 2007**

British Library Cataloguing in Publication Data:
A catalogue record for this book is available from the British Library

Printed by: Cromwell Press, Trowbridge
Cartography: Jonathan Young
Design: Sarah Labuhn
Edited by: Ian Howe

Front cover: Wherry and windmill
Back Cover top: Norwich Market
Back Cover bottom: Bigod's Castle

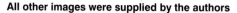

Picture Credits:
Front Cover: **Visit Norfolk**

Norfolk
Time to explore
www.visitnorfolk.co.uk

All other images were supplied by the authors

DISCLAIMER
While every care has been taken to ensure that the information in this guide
is as accurate as possible at the time of publication, the publisher and author
accept no responsibility for any loss, injury or inconvenience sustained by
anyone using this book.
